Publisher's Note

The book descriptions we ask booksellers to display prominently warn that this is an historic book with numerous typos, missing text or index and is not illustrated.

We scanned this book using character recognition software that includes an automated spell check. Our software is 99 percent accurate if the book is in good condition. However, we do understand that even one percent can be a very annoying number of typos! And sometimes all or part of a page is missing from our copy of a book. Or the paper may be so discolored from age that you can no longer read the type. Please accept our sincere apologies.

After we re-typeset and design a book, the page numbers change so the old index and table of contents no longer work. Therefore, we usually remove them.

Our books sell so few copies that you would have to pay hundreds of dollars to cover the cost of proof reading and fixing the typos, missing text and index. Therefore, whenever possible, we let our customers download a free copy of the original typo-free scanned book. Simply enter the barcode number from the back cover of the paperback in the Free Book form at www.general-books. net. You may also qualify for a free trial membership in our book club to download up to four books for free. Simply enter the barcode number from the back cover onto the membership form on the same page. The book club entitles you to select from more than a million books at no additional charge. Simply enter the title or subject onto the search form to find the books.

If you have any questions, could you please be so kind as to consult our Frequently Asked Questions page at www. general-books.net/faqs.cfm? You are also welcome to contact us there.

General Books LLC™, Memphis, USA, 2012. ISBN: 9780217183826.

Page *especially considered in the degrees of Parents, Children, Brothers, Sisters, Friends, Masters, Servants; and universal Philanthropy Jlriclly enjoined, as the basis of the Christian Religion. The whole concluding with a general Exhortation to Virtue* 191 DIALOGUE I.

MONDAY.

On Industry, Truth, and Sincerity.

Mentoria. AS your and your sister's improvement, mv dear Lady Mary, engrosses my whole attention, I propofe employing the remainder of the morning in pointing out thofe measures I think will be most conducive to it. I am not fo rigid as to exclude amusement from the system which I mean to form; though I wish but a small portion of your time to be spent in trifling pursuits. There is scarcely any thing of more importance, and what is more extraordinary, less attended to, than habitual Industry. So clearly am I convinced of the advantages which arise from the practice of this virtue, that in the profecution of my present plan, I intend to allow fome employ for every hour in the day, and shall endeavour to blend inB struction ssruction with amusement, as they do not appear to me the least incompatible, though from the prejudice of weak, minds, they are usually considered so. The thoughtless and inconsiderate receive instruction like a medicine, and nauseate the draught; but partake of the banquet of amusement, with as much ease and pleasure as if it were their daily sood. If we were to examine these different qualities with minute attention, we should find they often differ only in the name. Many pursuits where pleasure is the end propofed, produce disgust and pain; whilst on the contrary, thofe avocations which seem attended with difficulty, reward the labour of such who surmount them, with knowledge and glory!

Lady *Mary.*

My dear Mentoria, are we always to be reading, working, or writing, and never play? ', *Mentoria.*

Certainly not, my dear: my present oBject is to diversify your pursuits; and to regulate them in such a manner, that, whilst you are seeking improvement, you may be amused. The judicious choice and disposition of the agreeable and usesul qualifications of the mind, produce the fame effect in a human character as the contrast of light and shade, does in a fine picture, picture, which constitutes the beauty and intrinsic value of both.

Lady *Louisa.* I think we are always employed. How much time we spend in getting our lessons! I often lament I have not more time to play. *Mentoria.* I agree with you, Lady Louifa, in thinking you spend a great deal of your time in getting your lesfon: I am forry to add, as my opinion, often more than is necessary for the purpofe. The habitual Industry I mean to inculcate, will, I hope, obviate this objection, and give me no farther cause of complaint. When you serioufly reflect, that, is you do not persorm your business in the space of time appropriated to that purpofe, it will intersere with your attendance on your Masters, or fome other branch of your duty, you will be inclined to pursue your studies with the attention they deserve. The advantage would evidently be your own, as by that means, you would have part of your Ane entirely at your own dispofal. Lady *Mary.* What alteration then, my good Mentoria, do you mean to propofe in our education? *Mentoria.* None that will assect your Ladyship's peace. Ba I shall 1 shall expect never to see you idle: and shall be displeased, if you tell me you have nothing to do; always endeavour to suit your employ to the circumstances of your situation. I would advise, when you are engaged with your friends, to let your pursuit be of a nature that dees not require clofe application; as I thinkit a mark of ill breeding, to bestow great attention on any object, which does not immediately conduce to their amusement.

Lady *Louisa*..

I suppofe, as you are fo fond of reading, you will expect it to employ great part of our time. *Mentorifl*.

You are mistaken, my dear, I am no friend to perfons of your age spending much time in reading, except to thofe who are capable, and willing, to correct their errors. For though by Industry, you may comprehend the meaning of words, you can never attain the just pronunciation, but by the instruction of an intelligent mind.

Lady *Mary*.

I cannot yet discover, my dear Mentoria, in what you mean to differ from our usual mode os practice: Are we to be detained longer with you in the morning?

Mentoria. Mentoria.

It is not my intention to keep you one moment longer than the usual time. It is not the number of hours, but the use you make of them, which will secure your improvement. The mental, as well as the corporeal faculties, derive the most advantage from the sustenance which is administered in small quantities; the lighter the quality, the easier it is digested, and more conducive to the support and nourishment of the whole system.
Lady *Louisa*.

What are the peculiar advantages of Industry, my good Mentoria7 *Mentoria*.

They are of such general utility, it is impossible to enumerate them: thofe who are distinguished by any extraordinary qualities, are commonly indebted to this virtue for the superior excellence they have attained. Many usesul discoveries are produced by chance, which could never be brought to persection without the aid of Industry. I cannot produce a stronger instance to prove the esstcacy of Industry, than the advantages Demosthenes derived from this virtue. His, example.might to teach us, sew difficulties are insurmountable, for by nature he was not designed B 3 for for an Orator, as his voice was weak and inharmonious, and his manner ungracesul. Withv these desects, it is wondersul, he applied himself to the study of eloquence; as of all others it seemed the

least suited to his abilities. In order to remove the stammering articulation of his words, he used to declaim on different subjects with pebbles in his mouth, when he was ascending steep places, which strengthened his powers of respiration. To accustom himself to the noise of the Courts of Justice, he frequently made orations,by the sea-side, when? the waves were most tempestuous. He was no less attentive to his action, and general deportment; as he was conscious he had contracted a bad habit of shrugging up his shoulders, he caused a pulpit to be erected on such a particular construction, with an halberd hanging over it, in which he used to practise his declamations, that whenever the vehemence of his action prompted him to exceed the proper bounds, the halberd proved an-usesul monitor. His wisdom suggested to him the necessity of clofe application, he therefore had a study built under ground, where he used to seclude himself from the world, and often not appear for twa or three months. Whilst he waa was in this retirement, he shaved but one side of his head, that he might not be tempted to ap« pear in public.

Lady *Louisa*. I am astonished he had such resolution; I dare fay his friends used to laugh at him. *Mentoria*. The discouragement, my dear, he met with, enhances the merit of his perseverance; sor notwithstanding, on his first appearance he was received with univerfal difapprobation, and even silenced by the hisses of the populace, so far from discontinuing his pursuit, he redoubled his assiduity, and at last became one of the most eloquent men of the age. Lady *Louisa*. Do you think, my dear Madam, if I were to try and take great pains, I ssiould sing as well as Signora Sestini? *Mmtoria*. Try the experiment; always point out thofe as a model who excel; by which means you will acquire a tolerable degree of proficiency in the art you admire; though you may not be able to attain the fame degree of excellence. Lady *Mary*. I am surprised more persons do not sollow the good example of Demosthenes. *Mentoria. Mentoria.*

Few persons, my dear, are conscious of

their own desects. It is necessary to be sensible of the weakness of our flate, besore we can endeavour to sortify it. Thofe, whofe impersections are so glaring, cannot be ignorant of them, they turn their eyes from the dark side of the picture,and solace themselves, that they possess some usesul, or agreeable quality, which serves as a counterpoise sor thofe in which they are desective. There is another reason which may be alleged, why so sew endeavour industrioufly to excel; namely, the repugnance of human nature, to pursue any plan, to which it has not a natural propensity. There are scarcely any, who have resolution to act directly contrary to their inclination; and they urge in their desence, that the bent of the genius ought to be considered. To such persons I would reply, the initiation into all sciences and languages is tedious, and in some degree laborious: perseverance will enable us to gain the summit, which at our first view seem'd inaccessible. When we have attained thus far, we shall find the descent easy, and the path strewed with flowers, by the side of refreshing streams.

recollect a sew lines I wrote the other day on otr Industry, which I will now repeat, as they are applicable to my present purpofe.

Th' industrious bee extracts from ev'ry fiow'r It's fragrant sweets, and mild balfamic pow'r. Learn thence, with greatest care, and nicest skill. To take the good, and to reject the ill. By her example taught, enrich thy mind, Improve kind nature's gifts, by sense resin'd; Be thou the honey-comb in whom may dwell Each mental sweet, nor leave one vacant cell.

Lady *Louisa*. I hope, my dear Mentoria, I shall practise tlie excellent lesson, contained in thofe lines. What virtue do you esteem and recommend, next to Industry?

Mentoria. I purpofe now, my dear, to subjoin a sew observations on those, which ought to be the leading principle of your actions; I mean Truth and Sincerity, which, in many instances, are synonymous terms.

Lady *Mary*. My good Mentoria, pray,

what are synonymous terms?

Mentoria.

Words, which have a different sound, yet

B 5 bear

tear the fame signisication; such as *pit/ilia. nimity,* and *cowardice,* .with many others too tedious to mention.

Lady *Mary.* What resemblance is there between truth, and sincerity?

Mentoria. Truth is the mother of sincerity, who possesses all the amiable qualities of her excellent parent, and yields implicit obedience to her laws.

Lady *Louisa.* If I could not possess both these virtues, which ought I to chuse?

Mentoria. They are bound by such strong ties, it is impossible to disunite them; as wherever truth sixes her residence, sincerity is always found, her constant attendant.

Lady *Alary.* I have always been taught the necessity of speaking truth; and hope pever to err from it. *Mentoria.* I would earnestly advise yon, not only to avoid being guilty of advancing an abfolute falsehood, but also to guard against the flightest deviation from truth. In every system of laws, are specified different degrees of trespasses trespasses, and punishments annexed, proportionate to the offence committed. Thus, many perfons, who would shudder at the thought of being guilty of any violent asfault on the lives or properties of their sellow-crealures, make no scruple to injure them in a point, which more essentially affects their happiness. In like manner, many, who would he (hocked with the idea of openly violating the laws of truth, by telling a direct lye, make a constant practice of exteniating-fome circumstances, and exaggerating others, as best suits their purpofe. It is to this conduct, we are indebted for the mis-construction of most actions; the concealment of fome favourable incident osten produces the fame consequences, as the most full and elaborate consession of guilt. From which it evidently appears, we are bound by the strongest ties, to express every thing as it really is; neither to varnish a bad action with the weak excuse that it is a general practice, and, as such,

ought to be considered less atrocious: neither should our zeal in any cause, ever induce us to temporize, and give evidence against our judgment.

Lady *Louisa.* I suppose, my dear Mentoria, you would be B 6 extremely extremely displeased, is you discovered in roe an untruth.

Mentoria. It would give me infinite concern, my dear, as I should sear, it would give your friends an unsavourable opinion of you, and, in some degree, cast a stigma on your suture reputation. The path of truth is so wide and straight, I am surprized, any persons should preser the labyrinth of falsehood and deceit; as its windings are so intricate, that sew find their way out, though they have recourse to every artisice, to efsect their escape.

Lady *Mary.* It would mortify me exceedingly to have the, truth of what I advanced disputed. *Mentoria.* You are persectly right, my good Lady Mary; there cannot possibly be a more humiliating circumstance. I would wish your reputation for veracity to be so sirmly established, that your bare testimony would carry as strong convictions, as the most solemn protestations. In ordeP to avoid your honour being called in question, deal as little'as possible in the marvellous; nor ever affirm the truth of an improbable circumstance, without you faw the tranfaction, and are convinced of its reality.

There

There is another species of falsehood I shallparticularly guard you against, as it courts us under a pleasing sorm, and consequently blind our judgment: I mean the bad habit of repeating things as jokes, which have no soundation in truth; and also a supposition, that a falsity can be innocent, if it does not prejudice another. Thofe who indutge themselves in this practice, soon exceed the bounds which even their own imagination can allow to be innocent; as there are very sew so depraved, as to plunge at once into the depth of vice, but prc»ceed from a flight deviation from virtue, tcraa open violation and contempt of her laws.

Lady *Mary.*

I am certain, my dear Madam, what you have faid, will prevent my ever telling stories.

,' *Mentoria.*

I shall now proceed to point out the advantages, which arise from Sincerity. The practice of truth naturally produces this virtue; as thofe, who accustom themselves to make no promises, but what they intend to persorm, or not undertake what they think thfy cannot execute, never fail of possessing this amiable quality, which stamps-a value, and diffuses a sweetness over all their actions.

Lady *S* Lady *Louisa.* Lady *Mary.*

How are we to know, when people are sincere?

Mentoria. H" We are indispensibly bound to consider every body in that light, till they have given us just cause to be of a contrary opinion. It is more consistent with true charity, to deem a person innocent, till there is sull and clear conviction of his guilt. It would render our intercourse with society painsul, if we were to suspect the prosessions of our friends, and put an ill construction upon their kind offices. Common prudence sorbids our thinking, that every person, who treats us with civility and attention, is deeply interested in our welfare. Neither are we to take the flattering compliments of our acquaintance in a literal sense, as they too often are not the real sentiments of their hearts.

Lady *Mary.* Do not persons, who are sincere, always keep their word, and are they not constant in friendship?

Mentoria. Else they could not be esteemed sincere. It is necessary to insorm your Ladyship, there-are two kinds of promises; the one absolute, the the other conditional. The sormer ought to be persormed, though to our own prejudice or inconvenience; the latter, from intervening circumstances, may be postponed, and even annihilated. Respecting constancy in friendship, there requires little to be said, to evince the necessity of our being steady in our attachments, and faithful in our engagements. We should be cautious in the choice of our friends, and ever choofe to associate with thofe, who possess valuable, rather than shining qualities. Lady *Louisa.*

I suppofe, we should never sorfake our friends, whatever changes happen to take place in their situation.

Mentoria.

No alteration in their outward condition ought to lessen your affection sor them. On the contrary, if they labour under any affliction, or have selt any shock in their sortune, you should industrioufly seek every opportunity to convince them, they are hot of less consequence in your esteem. " You ought also to be more observant in paying them every mark of attention, than when they were your equals; lest they ascribe your negligence to pride, and consider it as an insult offered to their situation.

Lady

Lady *Mary.*

If any of my friends, my dear Mentorla-, were to act inconsistent with prudence, would it be blatneable to forfake them? *Mentorin.*

The bonds of friendship, under particular circumstances, may be broken, notwithstanding it is a serious and folemn engagement. For instance, if a young lady of your acquaintance was a notorious story-teller, or disobedient to her parents, I should not only think it a pardctnable, but a justisiable measure, to strike her from the list of your friends; as you arc no farther obliged to associate with a dangerous companion, than you would be required to visit her, if she were insected by the plague. As iii both cases, most probably the contagion would spread, the latter, would only endanger your constitution; whilst the former, prejudices what is insinitely of more importance, the reputation! Lady *Louisa.*

Are there any other duties, belonging to Sincerity*?* *Mentoria.*

TfSifi" keeping of secrets, is a branch of Sincerity, on which it is necessary for me to make a sew observations. You ought never to betray betray the trust repofed in you, or divulge any circumstances, your friend wishes to conceal; as nothing can render a person more contemptible, than breach ot' confidence. Lady *Mary.*

I suppofe, there would be no harm, if I told you only, the secrets, I was intrusted with. *Menioria.*

Your Ladyship will scarcely believe, notwithstanding you mean to pay me a compliment, that I should be extremely disgusted with you; and be apt to imagine, you would divulge my concerns to your young acquaintance. Whatever injunctions you lay me under not to speak of the anecdotes you had revealed, if I chofe to break through them, you could not with justice upbraid me as you had been guilty of the fame ofsence. I beg you will avoid reserve and duplicity, in your conduct. If your actions are regulated by the rules herein prescribed, concealment will be unnecesfary. Vanity, and self-importance, induce many persons to be treacherous, with no other view, than to increase their consequence: by which means, they TOunteract their own purpofe, in convincing us, they were unworthy the trust repofed in them; and ought to be shunned as traitors.

Lady

I vjplcy, my good Mentoria, you are *no* friepdtAsecrets.

"'-"' Mentoria.

No person can be less mysterious in their own concerns, than I am; though none can retain a secret more inviolably. If I think it prudent and sor the advantage of my friends, to conceal any circumstances or event of their lives, I do not require to be bound by promises, or any other ties; but am guided by the Christian principle, of " doing to others, as I would they should do unto me." Lady *Louisa.*

I hope, my dear Lady Mary, we shall both be exactly what good Mentoria wishes. Howrejoiced (he will be, to see us distinguished by the amiable qualities of Truth, Sincerity, and Industry. *Mentoria.*

Blend them with the three Christian virtues, Faith, Hope, and Charity; and on such a basis, you cannot fail to raise a fair temple, which you are indispensibly bound to dedicate to virtue.

Obey her disrates, at her altar bend; Convinc'd she is thy true, and surest friend.

Whene'er

"Whene'er in error's maze thou chance to stray.

Her voice recalls, and clears the doubtful way.

Directed thus by her unerring laws,.f Trace all thy blessings to their First Great Cause!

The great Creator wisely does dispense, Xo all his creatures, different kinds of sense:

To some he ministers the gifts to please, And pass thro' lise, with unaffected ease;

On others, kindly pours a depth prosound,

The darkest myst'ries clearly to expound.

Yet all are equal objects of his care, Each individual the undoubted heir Of suture bliss, prepar'dwith mighty love,

For all the righteous, in the realms above!

DIALOGUE II.

T U E S-D A Y.

On Orthography, and the Practical Use of Grammar.

Mentoria. MY dear Ladies, as you have gone through your disserent exercises entirely to my satisfaction; I shall now lay down some rules to accelerate your progress in English Gramr mar. As you have in the course of your lessons acquired the knowledge of Nouns, Pronouns, Adverbs, and Participles, it will be my present endeavour, to reduce them to a practical system. It is needless, to insorm your Ladyships, that those who are desective in Orthography, though in an exalted station of lise, are never ranked in the class of what is usually fliled stiled good company. Their elevation renders their impersections more conspicuous, and the reflection, that they have neglected to make a proper use of the opportunities granted them to improve their talents, subjects them to ridicule and contempt; whilst the poor, whose situation in lise excludes them from every source of mental cultivation, excite our pity, and demand our assistance As their ignorance cannot be imputed as a fault, the errors which are the natural consequence of it, should never be noticed, but from the humane motive of dispelling the darkness which obscures their understanding; This is a task of such a tender nature, it requires the hand of a skilsul artist to persorm the operation; lest, while we mean to heal, we wound.

Lady *Mary.*

I am much obliged to you, my dear Madam, sor the pains you take to improve me, and Lady Louifa; and hope by our assiduity, to.make you a suitable return. I am very desirous to speak and write correctly: The attention I pay to your instructions, I hope, will in a short time produce the desired effect. Lady *Louijg.*

My good Mentoria, I have sormed the fame resolution; which, I hope, will make amends for my former negligence.

Mentoria. Mentoria. If, my dears, your suture conduct will be consistent with your present declaration, I cannot doubt the advance of your improvement: your attainments will be the reward of my labours. Insancy like the Spring, is the time to sow the seed; which first blossoms, then comes to sull maturity, and at last decays. I hope the soil of your understanding is so sertile, and the culture so well attended to, the buds of Knowledge will expand besore the usual time, and be prematurely ripe.

Lady *Mary.* How rejoiced, my dear Mentoria, you will be, to see us more accomplished, than young ladies os our age usually are. *Mentoria.* I should be exceedingly mortified, to find you desective in any branch of your education. I think, at present there seems no probability of my suffering any inconvenience on that account. I will now pursue my scheme, and endeavour to make some observations on the use of Grammar; which, I hope, will be of future service to you. I shall begin, by supposing you in company with a litle girl about your own age; who would perhaps fay, "Pray, Lady Mary, when was you at the play?

Wheo When my Aunt and I *was* there, it was vafllv sull of company. Sir George and Lady Simple *dtsues* their compliments to you, and *hopes* you are

well, and *wishes* to know how *them* pretty flowers of yours *goes* on." I hear you reply, " My Governess, Miss Simple, teaches me, when I speak in or of the Plural, always to fay *were* instead of *was*: or is I address my discourse in the singular number, to make use of the words, *desires, fends, hopes, enquires, wishes,* &c. And when I speak of perfons, she directs me to fay, *they, those, them, who, whom;* but when I mention inanimate things, always to substitute the word *which* for *whom. Examples.* To *whom* do you speak? Or *who* told you fo? Are *those* things yours? *Which* of these apples do you choofe?" Lady *Louisa.*

I clearly comprehend these examples; but wish to know the distinction of *these,* and *those. Mentoria.*

I will readily comply with your request. The term *these* implies possession. Example. *"These* flowers in my hand:" and is often used to express the present time, as in this instance, In *these* days of resinement: whilst *those* is a word relative, or tiled in reserence to fome distant object; as *those* books on the table: and and is frequently used to denote a past transaction. Example.— " In *those* early dnys, superstition prevailed." I shall now proceed to explain the words, *hence, thence,* and *whence,* and their connection with *here, there,* and *where.* For instance, Whilst I am *here,* I will ride; but when I go from *hence,* I will walk. I intend to read the Spectators, when I am *there*; but when I go from *thence,* I propofe to embroider a sire-screen. From *whence* did you bring this? Which implies, *Where* did you meet with it? Take this bird to the nest, from *whence* it came: which signisies, *Where* it came from. I shall conclude this dissertation by enquiring, whether you remember the Epicene nouns.

Lady *Mary.* Are they not thofe which may with equal propriety be applied to the Masculine and Feminine Gender? *Mentoria.* You are persectly right, as to the general idea. I shall enumerate a sew particular instances; which I hope, will enable you to form a competent knowledge of this branch of Grammar.

Example, The terms, Parent, Children, Friend, Neighbour, Cousin, Servant, are all Epicenes.

C Lac'y Lady *Louisa.*

My dear Mentoria, nothing can be more dear. Lord and Lady H. are my Parents, Lord George and myself are tlieir Children. The Duke and Dutchess of D. are my friends, Sir Charles and Lady F. my neighbours; Lord William and Lady Frances S. my Cousins, and Thomas and Kitty, Servants. *Mentoria.*

It gives me great pleasure to sind your Lady ship fo attentive to my instructions: you could not possibly have given me a stronger proof of your prositing by them, than the just comparifon you have drawn. Lady *Louisa.*

I hope I shall foon be able to express myself with great accuracy. I air. sure, nry good Mentoria, you will learn me to speak and write just as I ought. *Mentoria.*

There requires nothing more to produce this happy change, than a sixed determination to observe and imitate the converfation and conduct of thofe, who are eminent for their great attainments. You were guilty of a palpable mistake in the speech you have just made. You faid, I should *karn* you to speak well: when when in reality, the instructor *teiches,* and the scholar *learns.* I shall beg you for the suture, to attend to this distinction. Persection in any art or science, is not easily attained: you must not imagine you have gotten to your journey's end, when in reality you are advanced but a sew paces; yet be encouraged by the pleasing assurance, that every step you take, removes you farther from ignorance, and will at last conduct you to the goal of wisdom! Lady *Mary.* As you have frequently enjoined me to ask the meaning of every word I do not comprehend, I beg you will insorm me what Science is?

Mentoria. Your Ladyship has anticipated my intention; as it was my fixed purpofe to reserve the discussion of that point to some suture opportunity. A laconic or concise answer must suffice for the present; as I intend to subjoin a sew remarks on the articulation of letters and words, and also point out some capital mistakes, as they appear to me necessary appendages to the soregoing observations. Science is a general-term. sor all human learning; though when annexed to the idea of Arts, is C 2 confined consined to thofe taught in the universities,

or other seminaries of learning; such as grammar, astronomy, logic, rhetoric, arithmetic, geometry, and music.

Lady *Louisa.*

My dear Mentoria, as you are going to enumerate errors in speech, I suppofe, Miss

Simple will surnish you with many examples.

I observed, the last time I was in company with her, she pronounced many words wholly disferent from what I am taught.

Mentoria.

I suppofe, my dear, she has not been instructed at all; or, what is still worse, probably flighted the admonitions of her Governess, who might, notwithstanding, be a sensible, well-bred woman. I have observed, amongst many other errors, she always fays *perdigious,* instead of *prodigious;* or is she means to describe a perfon of an open and candid disposition, she expresses herself by the word *ingenious;* which she mistakes for *ingenuous.* If she describes an outrageous perfon, flie favs, They are *cbflropolous,* instead of *ebjlrtperous.* Speaking of a venomous creature, she faid, it was an *obnoxious* animal; which she mistook for the word *noxious,* which signisies the being hurtsul 4T hurtsul in its nature; the term *obnoxious* only implying,the being liable, or subject to any thing. Whenever she talks of a person in a weak state, who is obliged to be dieted, (he fays, he is reduced to a *regiment,* instead of *regimen.* If she intends to describe the usual methods, which are taken to bring an ofsender to justice, she insorms you, he is *persecuted.* She is totally ignorant, the word *persecute* is improperly applied, except to express the hardships many have undergone, in desence of their religious principles; and does not, in the lest, convey the idea of a legal *prosecution* Lady *Mary.*

I often blush sor her, when she pretends to speak French j as she generally pronounces it improperly.

Mentoria.

I have heard her frequently fay *bone mott,* for *bon mot; sox pass,* for *faux pas.* Or if she meets with the word *corps,* which signifies a collective body of men, she calls it *corpse,* which, in English, means a dead body. The other da, she was describing a fracas, or disturbance, which had happened in the family; which she declared was the *v/orR.sraca/s,* she had ever seen.

C 3 Lady Lady *Louisa.*

Upon my word, my dear Madam, the errors of Miss Simple's converfation appear to me in fo difagreeable a light, I do not think I shall ever take pleasure in her company. Whenever I hear her speak, I shall endeavour to correct her errors.

Mentoria.

Your intention, my dear Lady Louifa, is very good; yet. I would ever wish you to avoid a conscious superiority. A degree of modest difsidence should attend all your actions. Whenever you give your opinion, (which, at your age, ought never to be done unaskedj you should deliver your sentiments with deserence to thofe of superior judgment. This turn of mind will not obscure ypur merit, as modesty adds a grace to every other virtue.

The modest snow-drop, emblem of fair truth,

Conveys a lesson to the thoughtless youth;

That unassuming worth will ever sind

A warm reception, in a geri'rous mind!

Lady *Mary.*

My dear Mentoria, I suppofe you will now

give give some directions, how the different letters are to be articulated. When two confonants precede a vowel, that, which joins to the vowel forms the found, as in the word *Ptolomy,* which is read *Tolomy:* as alfo *Czar,* the title of the Emperor of Russia, usually called the *Zar.* I shall now specify a sew instances, where the *H* is mute; as in the word *chart,* whichj signisies a map, and should be pronounced *cart.* The words

chaos, and *chalybeate,* are subject to the fame rule; as alfo *magna charta,* which is the law that constitutes the freedom of the English nation. When two letters of the fame fort join, the sirst is generally founded hard; as in *access, accept, accelerate.* An exception to this rule is evident, in the words *accord, accuse,* and *accumulate.* When an TV follows an As, the found of the TV is wholly lost; as in *hymn, condemn,* &c. If a *G* precedes *N,* the former bears no part in the found; which is evinced in the words *malign, benign, reign,* and *feign.* When an *H* follows a *P,* they neither of them preserve their natural found, but are compounded into that of the letter *F;* as *physician, phosphorus,* and*philosopher,* I will not, my dear, at present, give any other instance, to ensorce what I have already faid; fo shall *Mentoria.* I will endeavour to express my sentiments as concise as possible, aud never use technical terms, but when they are absolutely necesfary. Lady *Louisa.* Pray, what are technical terms, my dear Mentoria? I never heard ot them besore. *Mentoria.* They are thofe terms, which belong to any particular art or science. A knowledge of which cannot be acquired, but by applying diligently to the arts; or attention to the conversation of thofe, who are conversant in them. The language of an architect, painter, or mathematician, would appear unintelligible to you: yet no other words would so well express their meaning. Lady *Mary.* Now, my good Mentoria, pursue your plan. *Mentoria.* I shall begin, by insorming you of the use of Dipthongs. Example. Æsop is to be read Esop; as the double letter takes the sound of the single *E.* The words *Oedipus,* and *Otconomv,* are pronounced agreeable to the fame rule. C 4 When now now dismiss you, with an exhortation to retain thofe, I have just recited; which will induce me to enlarge soon on this, or any other subject: so adieu!

Lady *Louisa.* PRAY, my dear Mentoria, what is to be the subject of your instructions this morning?

Mentoria. I really have not determined that point; but believe, they will chiesly consist of reflections, that will naturally arise, from whatever engages our attention. Lady *Mary.* I have a great favour to aik my good Mentoria, but have scarcely courage to tell you what it is: yet I think you-would be inclined to grant it. *Mentoria. Mentoriam* Why fliould your LadysnTpTcruple to make your requests known?: There are very few improper, if they are presented with modest diffidence, and in deserence to superior judgment. This turn of mind the French call *mauvaise honte,* which signisies false shame; from which I would wish you wholly exempt. I am ever inclined to promote your amusement; and dare fay, in the present instance I shall have no cause to reject your petition.

Lady *Mary.*

To keep you no longer in suspense, Lady Louifa and myself wish you would permit Lady Jane Placid, and Lady Ann Sprightly, to spend a day with us.

Mentoria.

So this, my dear Lady Mary, was the mighty asfair, you could not summon courage to utter! I not only give my consent to it, because I do not difapprove of it, but froYn the stronger inducement, of wishing you to form an intimacy with them; as they are the kind of companions, I wish you to asfociate with. Lady *Louisa.*

Which do you like best, my dear Mentoria, Lady Jane Placid, or Lady Ann Sprightly?

Mentoria 1 Mentoria,

Their qualities are so very disferent, it is difficult to determine, which is the most worthy of admirations They both possess great merit, though in such a different line, they will not admit of a comparison; as Lady Ann's vivacity enlivens Lady Jane's compofure and serenity; and Lady Jane's complacency keeps Lady Ann's cheersulness within proper bounds. Thus you see, they both derive advantage from the contrast which is sound in their characters.

Lady *Mary.*

May we invite Miss Simple the fame day?

Mentoria.

By no means: you should always endeavour to sorm your party of such persons, whofe sen timents and pursuits are suppofed to agree. Lady Frances Trifle, and Lady Betty Hoyden will be more suitable to Miss Simple. Lady *Louisa.*

How shall we divert ourselves. my dear Mentoria? I hope, you will give me leave to make tea.

Mentoria. 'ii. You must regulate your own amusements, and persorm the duties of the table, both at dinner and tea; as I shall spend the day out, "j that that I may not check, your mirjh; which, I hope, will not exceed the bounds of good sense and politeness.

Lady *Mary.* I am afraid, my dear Mentoria, we shall be very uncomfortable without you; and be at a bofs, how to entertain our guests. *Mentoria.* To obviate this objection, I shall lay down a sew rules, to regulate your conduct on this, and future occasions. Refinement in manners, is the only quality which can distinguish you' irom the lower class os-people; as sincerity, benevolence, and many other virtues, are not confined to any particular station in lise: though politeness, or what is usually called good breeding, is never possessed but by thofe whofe understandings are cultivated, and their manners sormed by the society of polite, wellbred persons.

Lady *Louisa.* Will the keeping company with polite people make me the fame?

Mentoria.

Unless it is your Ladyship's own fault, by obstinately persisting in your errors; or by inattention, the neglefcling to make observations on the manners you ought to imitate. This k&d kind of conduct undoubtedly would prevent your making any improvement, and would be as absurd, as if you were to shut your eyes at an exhibition of sine pictures; which would prevent your drawing any copy trom the originals.

Lady *Mary.* Pray, my dear Mentoria, instruct us how to behave the whole day. I should be very forry, is we spoke or acted improperly to Lady Jane, cr Lady Ann, when they savour us with their company.

Mentoria. It is scarcely possible, to form a settled plan for behaviour, as there are fo many circumstances, on which the propriety of it depends: fo that it can only be regulated by good sense and discretion, which will ever dictate what is proper to be persormed on every occasion. But notwithstanding I cannot reduce politeness to a regular system, I will endeavour to point out a sew of its essential qualities. Lady *Louisa.* How should we receive our visitors, my good Mentoria? *Mentoria.* You should endeavour to express, how happy you are to see them; that you have thought it it long, since you had last that pleasure. You should then enquire after their own health, and that of every branch of their family: and if any have been ill, congratulate them on their recovery. Respecting amusements you should never consult your own inclination, but always let thofe of your guests take the lead; and never raise trifling objections, to any they propofe. As their entertainment is the chies object, you should readily comply with whatever seems conducive to it. It would make you appear petulant, as well as unpolite, if, when they expressed a desire to play at Questions and Commands, you seemed discontented, and declared a preserence to play at Blindman's-Buff. It is also incumbent on you, to check any little disputes, between your younger sisters and brothers; and so far from taking the least part in them, you should wholly suppress them. This conduct will make you appear in an amiable light, and give Lady Jane and Lady Ann a favourable impression of you.

Lady *Mary.* I hope, by the help of your kind instructions, we shall behave with propriety, particularly at dinner time.

Mentoria. Mentoria. Do not suffer your attention to your guefls so wholly to take up your thoughts, as to make you sorgetful of the superior obligations, you owe to your Creator: return him thanks for the blessings he has already granted, and implore his suture mercies, besore you partake of the repast, his Providence has afforded you. When this duty is persormed, help your friends to thofe' parts you think best, and which, in general, seem in the highest estimation. Let the attention you pay them, prevent their requesting to be helped to any particular dish. If they express their approbation, and seem to give a preserence to' any part of the entertainment, you should request them to testify how much they like it, by eating some more of it. But is they decline your intreaties, do not repeat them; as persons, who are accustomed to good company seem as much at their ease, when they dine out, as when they are at home, and take it sor granted, they are as welcome in their friend's house, as their friend would be in theirs. 'I would advise you, at your own, or at any other table, never to choose those things, that are rarities, Wf-Spr of which there seems but a small quantity: though though I would wish this denial not to be visible, lest it occasion compliments, and give pain to those, who have chosen the things you resused. There is another circumstance, I shall mention, which is, never to be warm in the praise of your own victuals, or ever mention what they cost. Alfo, when the dinner disappears, never make it the subject of your conversation: the excellence of a pie, or pudding, should never be extolled, but when it is on your plate; as, at the most, they deserve but sew commendations. Let me intreat you, to close your meal with thanksgiving and praise to the great Cause, from whence it proceeded; which will inspire your mind with ease and cheersulness. Lady *Louisa*-. But what shall we talk of, my dear Mentoria, when dinner is over? *Mentoria*. That does not wholly depend on your Ladyship, as conversation consists ol the sentiments of different perfons, mutually expressed, without reserve. Some have the gift of enlivening this pleasing intercourse, by the brilliancy os their wit; others add a grace to it, by the depth of their judgment: whilst there are are many, who possess no extraordinary qualifications, yet are, nevertheless, pleasing companions; because they are converfant in the affairs of the world, or pay attention toothers. Lady *Mary*. ample matter sor converfation, and enable you to pass yc ur time agreeably.

Ought I, my dear Memorise to enquire what work they are about, what books they have read, or where they have been? *Mentoria*.

Yes, my dear, though the bare reply to these questions ought not to fatisfy your Ladyship. When you are insormed of their different pursuits, enquire how far they are advanced in their embroidery; and whether they think it possible you could execute a piece of the fame nature. Respecting books, you should express a desire to know their opinion of those they have read, as well as yourself, to find if their sentiments correspond with your own; and also of new publications, and authors to which you are a stranger: that by their account you may sorm an idea whether they would improve or entertain you. In 'the recital of what they had seen, or where they had been, you would naturally be led to enquire into the different situation of the places; which they liked best, and on what account they gave the preference. These enquiries will surnish ample

Lady *Louisa*. —

I have observed many people tiresome in their converfation, and not the least entertaining *Mentoria*.

I have met with many in the course ps lise, who may not unjustly be compared to a pump, from which the water is drawn with difficulty; arid also with others, who, from their pleasing volubility, may be compared with equal propriety to a slowing river. Lady *Mary*.

I shall also tell them what lessons we learn; and enquire whether they are taught theiame. *Mentoria*.

I am pleased, my dear Lady Mary, to find you are desirous to sorm a degree of comparison between their improvement and yours; as it will excite emulation, and create in your mind a strong desire to make a rapid progress in your learning. For my own part, if I were a little girl, nothing would mortify me so much as the being-remarkably backward of my age; a tall girl is more particularly bound to hasten her improvement, as persons in general form great expectations from her external ap pearance, and are extremely disappointed to j find an insant mind, in almost a

woman's body; expressing their astonishment in the sollowing terms; " What pity it is so large a casket "should contain such a bauble!" Lady *Mary*. Do you think, my good Mentoria, my mind is a bauble!

Mentoria. You should never, my dear, suppofe yourself the person pointed at in any general observation; as it is a maxim of true politeness to exempt the present company from any personal reflection. The intrinsic value of your mind, depends on the care you take to embellissi and adorn it. Like the diamond in its natural state, it is unpolissied; the one deriyes its lustre from the skill of the lapidarv, the other from education.

Lady *Lout/a*, I have a great inclination, my dear Madam, to give Lady Jane Placid one of my pretty trinkets; I am sure she will like it, it is so beautiful.

Mentoria. I have not the least objection: but would advise your Ladyship not to enumerate its beauties when you present it; but rather tell her it is a trifle, and not worth her acceptance; yet you hope (he will receive it as a token of affection. You should never enhance the value.of any favour you conser; but always endeavour to point out the persections, and increase the worth of thofe you receive. The mention of benefits reminds me to warn you, not to speajc of thofe you conser, besore, or to the person, on whom they were bestowed: as it entirely cancels the.obligation, and clearly indicates you persormed the service more from ostentation than friendship! Lady *Louisa*. 1 will never, sor the suture, (peak to my servant of any favour she receives from me. I used to be perpetually telling her what returns *1* expected sor my kindness, and never thought she could do enough sor me! *Mentoria*.

To convince you how different my sentiments are in this respect, I never exact, or even wish a return sor any service I persorm; though I endeavour in every instance to testify my gratitude to thofe persons who have obliged me.

Lady *Mary*.

I hope, my dear Mentoria, I shall acquit myself properly at the tea table; I shall be less at at a lofs, because I have often made tea sor you.

Mentoria. I make no doubt your guests will be persectly fatisfied, as a wish to please, generally produces the desired effect. Attend to the necesfary forms; and endeavour to make the tea agreeable to their taste: you must also be caresul not to flop the table, overset the urn, or be guilty of any thing to cause consusion and disturbance.

Lady *Louisa.* That would be a fad affair, as it would turn all our joy into sorrow! but how, my d ar Madam, are we to be employed after we have drank tea?

Mentoria. You should propofe several kinds of amusements, and when the ladies have determined the choice, pursue it without deliberation, for fear their carriage should setch them when you are in the height of your diversion; which might perhaps oblige you to leave it. Lady *Mary.* How must I take leave of them: I am sine I shall be sorry to part with friends I so much esteem. *MinMentoria.*

Your seelings will suggest to your Ladyship the best mode of expressing them, which I should suppofe will be to this effect: that you regretted being deprived of their company so early, and that you had no idea it was so late, you had been so happy in their converfation. You should also desire them to present your love, or compliments, to every part of their family.

Lady *Mary,*

I think, my good Mentoria, you seem to have regulated our conduct, from the time of the ladies coming into the house, to their departure from it, by your kind instructions. *Mentoria.*

Yet it may not be unusesul if I extend them a little farther, to direct your behaviour after they are gone. Nothing is more usual or disgusting, than to see persons of all ranks and degrees, criticise on the dress and general deportment of their departed guests; and often ridicule and condemn thofe things behind their back, which, to their face, they approved or applauded. Let me intreat you never to make your friends appear in a difadvantageous light, but, on the contrary, extol the persections tions

and accomplishments they possess, and cast a veil over their desects. Lady *Loui/a.* I shall observe this rule, never to make a jest of any perfon, particularly of thofe with whom I live on terms of friendship.. *Mentoria.* I hope your Ladyship will keep to this excellent refolution; for my own part, when I see people wounding the reputation of their friends, I always expect to come in (or mv share os the general flaughter. Nothing but arrogance, and an exalted idea of our own consequence, can shield us from this sear; as there is no character fo persect, but what there can be fome fault or weakness discovered in it, which like the spots in the sun (if viewed through a proper medium) do not take from its radiant lustre.

Lady *Mary.* I did. not know there were any spots in the fun, my dear Mentoria.

Mentoria. We can perceive them very dearly by the help of a telescope; as to pursue the simile, by the aid of discernment, we discover the blemishes of the human mind,

D Lady

Lady *Louisa.* Why, my dear madam, do you compare die sun to our understandings? *Mcntoria.* For these reasons, they are respectively the most glorious works of the creation, and often Jhine with resplendence, though they are sometimes obscured by cloudsLady *Mary* What clouds can possibly affect the mind, and take from its lustre?

Mcntoria. Thofe of ignorance, prejudice, superstition, and every other quality which makes us deviate from our duty, or impedes our pursuing any laudable purpofe.

Lady *Louisa.* Pray, Mentoria, what is the distinction between Politeness and Civility? *Mentoria.* There is a very essential difference, and. mav be defined thus: civility consists of good osfices persormed by impulse or instinct, whilst thofe which are classed under the rank of politeness, are produced by reflection, and proceed more from the head than the heart. Lady *Mary.* Mav a person be extremely civil who hrs not the least pretensions to politeness?

Mentoria. Mentoria.

Undoubtedly; a ploughman may possess civility in the highest degree. When he takes off his hat as your Ladyship passes, or moves a hurdle to facilitate your getting over a stile; he acts as much in character, and renders you as substantial a service, as a sine gentleman would, by handing you into your carriage, though you ought to express your acknowledgement in very different terms. Lady *Louisa.*

In what else do these agreeable qualities differ?

Mentoria.

It often happens the distinction does not arise from the difference of the actions themselves; but proceeds only from the superior grace with which thofe of politeness are performed. If we trace minutely the various operations of lise, we shall find in general, thofe in a high and low state, are employed in nearly the same pursuits, are impelled by the fame motives, and differ not so much in the plan as in the execution of their scheme. They talk, read, walk, eat, and persorm every sunction allowed to human nature; yet what a different effect they produce? they scarcely seem to admit of a comparison.

D 2 The

The discourse of a clown, does not found like the fame language,, with that which flows from the lips of an orator; neither does his ungracesul step appear to be produced from-the use of the fame organs, which charm us in the gracesul motion of a well-bred man or woman: to clofe the comparison, how essentially the uncouth and hasty meal of the farmer, differs from the luxurious and elegant repast of the fine gentleman; the one is regulated in his actions by nature, which produces civility; the other by refinement, which constitutes politeness. To pursue my usual plan of preserring mediocrity in all things, I wish thofe with whom I associate to have a portion of these different qualities blended in their characters; that from nature they may derive sincerity, and from refinement, thofe graces which are its best ornaments! Lady *Mary.*

I hope, my dear madam, by my care and assiduity, to reward you for the pains you take with me. Is not Gratitude an amiable, quality?

Mtntoria.

Certainly, my dear, it is a virtue which ought to be cherished, as it is but seldom practised. The generality of she world content themselves themselves with the bare acknowledgment of an obligation, and, scarcely ever seek an opportunity to return it, which is the more extraordinary, as it is a debt every one has power to pay, which Milton thus expresses: " A grateful "mind, by owing owes not, but still pays, "at once indebted and discharged!" which implies, gratitude is the only tribute required, when it is not in your power to make a more substantial return sor any benefit received.

Lady *Luuisd.*

If acts of gratitude are so easily persormed, I am surprized they are not more frequently practised.

Mentoria.

Persons in general are so eager in the pursuit of benefits, they no sooner gain one, than they seek to obtain another, which scarcely leaves them leisure for the exercise of this virtue; and also when they are possessed of the advantage, are too apt to sorget the means by which it was acquired. As I know you are sond of poetry, I will repeat an invocation to gratitude, which I wrote some days ago.

Hail, gratitude divine, of heav'nly birth! Whence art thou sound, a sugitive on earth? Where is thy dwelling,, art thou doom'd to roam. From pole to pole? yet find sto. friendly dome D. & To.

S

To shelter thee from insult, and from pride
Will no kind breast thy gries and cares divide?
Ill-fated maid, thy votaries withdraw,
Deny allegiance to thy facred law.
Thy spotless altars, no oblations grace;
Thy favours wrote on fand the winds efface.
What tho' but few attend thy exil'd fate,.
Thou'rt freed from pomp,, and vain parade of
(state. Design but to hear thy modest

suppliant's pray r, Let her thy silken bands sor ever wear!

Lady *Mary.*

My dear Mentoria, I thank you for reciting thofe lines; but shall be more obliged, if you will explain them.

Mentoria.

It will give me pleasure, my dear Lady Mary, to point out the different allusions which they contain; as it will enable you to comprehend the sense of the invocation. The supposition that gratitude is of celestial birth, denotes the divinity of her nature; and the idea of her being a sugitive, sully expresses she is a wanderer from her native country. The passage: 111 fated maid, thy votaries withdraw, Deny allegiance to thy facred law!

Thy

Thy spotless altars, no oblations grace;

Thy favours wrote on fand, the winds efface.'

Imply, that thofe who are bound by the strongest; obligations, frequently neglect to. jtiake their proper acknowledgments, and resuse to pay the tribute which is due; alfo that the favours we receive, make but a flight impression on our hearts, and are often erased by scenes of folly and dissipation, which are in their nature as light as air. The concluding lines

Deign but to hear thy modest suppliant's pray 7, Let her thy silken bands for ever wear:

Clearly indicate mv ardent desire to be guided by this divine virtue, whofe yoke is easy, anil burthen light, and of whom with propriety it may be said, her service is persect freedom. Lady *Louijh.* from your description, my dear Mentorij, gratitude seems to be but in an uncomfortable situation, as she has no habitation; and is obliged to wander far from her native-country to seek an abode.

Mentoria. Let her then sind an asylum in your breast; make frequent oblations at her shrine, which D 4 must mull consist of univerfal charity and benevolence, as no other facrisice k acceptable to her. Yield implicit obedience to her laws, bind yourself with her silken

cords, and preser them to the setters of guilt, or the shackles of folly. Lady *Alary.*

My dear Lady Louifa, we will,, both, of us, fee votaries of gratitude, which shall be testisied by duty to our parents, and respect to good Mentoria, for the pains she takes to improve us.

Mentoria.

Exclusive of the advantage I shall derive from the practice of this refolution, I rejoice in it, because it will influence your whole conduct, and regulate the actions of your suture lise. The duration of a building depend entirely on-the strufiure of the foundation: if the basis be not sirm, the edisice soon falls tew decay, which evinces the necessity in the forjnation of a hutn.an character, to erect the fabric ori the folid, and immutable principles of virtue and religion. Thofe who preser supersicial accomplishments to these divine attributes, may be compared to the foolish man described in the gofpel, who buik his house on the sand, which when the wind arofe, and the rains descended, beat upon, the house and it sell, and and great was the fall thereof. The simile may be defined thus: that thofe of unenlightened minds, are not sortified against the storms of affliction; nor are they able to surmount the difficulties they meet with in their warsare upon earth. The great fall of the building, denotes how transient and temporary all hopes of happiness prove, except thofe which-axe fouiidedon. religion and virtue.

DIALOGUE IV. THURSDAY. On Elocution and Geography. *Mentoria.* BEFORE I begin the business allotted for this morning, I shall congratulate you on your brother's arrival from Harrow, and beg the favour of Lady Louifa to insorm him, I shall be extremely glad of his company, which undoubtedly will be an addition to your happiness.

Lady *Louisa.* My dear Mentoria, I will setch him this moment; as I know he will rejoice to join our party. (Lady L. returns, introducing' her brother Losd *George.)* You cannot imagine, my dear Mentoria, how rejoiced Lord George was to ccme, and he would bring his books to read to you.

D *6 Men/oria, Mentoria.* I thought it might be agreeable to your. Lortfship to spend fome of your leisure hours with your sisters, which indticed me to request the favour of your company-1 will join with them in endeavouring to make the holidays as cheerful to you as possible. I hope, you will not think it lessens your consequence as a man, tot be taught by a Governess,, and have young Ladies for your school-sellows and companions. Lord *George* Not in the least, Madam: I shall esteem myself much obliged to you, for permitting me topartake of your instructions.. *Mentoria.* Pray, my Lord, who is your-particular frienÆ at school? Do any of Miss Simple's brothers or cousins go to Harrow? The samily of the Simples are fo numerous, I think wherever one goes, there is fome branch of it. Lord *George.* I recollect several of that name - but he wliois the most remarkable, is Sir Simon Simple,, cousin to the Miss Simple you know. *Mentoria.* By what quality is he fo particularly distinguished? I sear, by none that do him credit.

Lord

Lord *George.* When we are conning our lessons be is playing at marbles, fo that when his master is to hear his task, he cannot say it, for whkh he gets flogged;. and when we are at play, be is blubbering and crying, with a fool's cap on his head.

Lady *Louisa..* How I should laugh at him, and compare him. to Midas with his asses ear. Lady *Mary.* I wish your Lordship could recollect anymore instances ot Sir Simon's folly. Lord *George.* You cannot imagine how diverting it is to hear him read: It is just like the tolling of a bell, he goes Ding, Dong, Dong! and lays sach a stress on, *and, the, to,* and all monofyllables, that his Master has scarcely patience to hear him.

Mentoriax I am not surprised at that,, as nothing can bemore tirefome than to hear a perfon read ill, and it is impossible to read well, without entering into the subject; but from your account, I take it for granted, Sir Simon has not sense enough to be deeply interested in any History. The enly method to read,

with propriety, is to observe serve the stops with great attention; and *to* avoid a monotony, as much as possible, by acquiring a proper cadence and modulation of the voice. Lady *Mary.* What is Monotony, my dear Mentoria? *Mentoria. I* can venture to pronounce your Ladyship isno stranger to the thing itself,, though you are to the term which expresses it. It signisies the reading in one continued tone of voice; which is produced by neglecting to vary it, as the subject require?. Nothing can be more absurd than this stile of reading, as you should always endeavour *to* express the sense of the Author, and deliver his sentiments with as much ease and feeling, as if they were your own.

Lady *Louisa.* I wish I could attain this degree of persection. » *Mentoria.* Simple narrative is the easiest kind of reading for young beginners; as it requires but little elevation and change of voice. Lady *Mary.* Pray, my dear Madam, what do you mean' *by* simple narrative *Mentoria, Mentoria.* It is the recital of mere matter of fact; and consists in expressing in a natural and easy stile,, the occurrences incident to human lise. Lady *Louisa.* What is the most difsicult to read well?

Mentoria. Thofe compofitions which abound with invocations, exclamations, and frequent interrogations; as they require to be read with dignity and grace. Lady *Mary.* I wish to know the meaning of invocations. I remember your repeating one on Gratitude. *Mentoria.* They are of several kinds, and consist inimploring the aid and assistance of a superior Power; they may be ranked in the following classes. Thofe addressed to the Deity—of which I shall produce an example from Thompfon. "Father of Light and Lise, thou good Supreme, "O teach me what is good, teach me Thyself!" The next are thofe presented to Apollo, the Muses, ©rany Virtue,, and are used by Poets to give a grace to their Compositions; and often to apologize for their want of abilities, which is manisested, by their desiring to be inspi. ed with the gift of Poesy. To give you a clear idea idea of this poetic siction, I shall repeat a sewlines from a letter I

sent some time since to a. friend; in which I invoked the Muse Clio, in the sollowing words:

Hail, gentle Clio! sorm the verse
In numbers musical, and terse;
Diffuse thy softness o'er each line, friendship and Truth with grace combines'

Lady *Alary.*

I clearly comprehend the disserent qualitiesef these invocations; but pray, what are excfcumations?

Merit aria.

They denote surprize or astonishment; and' eften express our admiration of any extraordinary person, or tiling. Such is the sollowing instance,, which is part of the panegyric bestowed on Great Britain, in Thomson's Sea sons:

Heavens! what-agoodly prospect spreads around,, ©fhills, and dales, and woods, and lawns, and spires, And glittering towns, and gilded streams,_till all The stretching landscape into smoke decays! '. Lady.

Lady *Louisa.* We have now heard every part explained, except interrogation. *Men/eria.* There requires little to be said on this subject, as you cannot be ignorant, that to interrogate, is to question. I will however conclude this dissertation, with an example from Pope:

What, if the soot, ordained the dust to tread, Or hand to toil, aspir'd to be the head? What is the head, the eye.the ear, repin'd To serve, mere engines, to the ruling mind?

Lady *Mary.* I admire the instance you have produced, and shall take the liberty, my good Mentoria, to remind you os a promise you made yesterday.

Menteria. I recollect, and will instantly comply with, it: Was it not to insorm you of the nature of Geography? Lady *Alary.* Yes, my dear Madam, and I am all impatience till you begin.

Mentoria.

Geography teaches you the form of the Earth,, Earth, and the situation of each particular part os it. You are not ignorant, the World is round, and consists of Seas, Continents, Iflands, Peninsulas, Rivers, Promontories/ Rocks, and Mountains. In order to give you a clear idea of the Rudiments of Geography, preparatory to your being regularly taught, I shall endeavour to explain these disferent branches, and then proceed to enlarge on other parts of this usesul Science. The Ocean is the main Sea, the depth and extent of which is past our finite comprehension. The principal Seas I can recollect are the Mediterranean, Baltic, Euxine, and Adriatic. The Cont'nent is a vast united tract of Land, over which it is practicable to travel from one place to another: as sor instance, from France to Germany, Italy, Spain, Portugal, Turkey, or even India, by pasting over the deserts of Arabia; but this last is very dangerous, not only from the probability of meeting with the wild Arabs,. and noxious animals, but also from the wind rising to a considerable height, which istlways of fatal consequence to travellers, as the clouds of land either prevent their pursuing the right course, or frequently blind them, and sometimes totally overwhelms them.

Lady

Lady *Louisa.* Pray, what is an Ifland? My brother, I dare fay, knows?

Mentoria. Ifland is a general term for every tiling encompassed by water. In the more elevated, sense, it signisies any habitable place or Kingdom, surrounded by the sea, as Great Britain or Ireland. The advantages arising from this situation are evidently these; the convenience ot importing into every part of it, the produce of other countries; and to thofe engaged in commerce, the equal advantage of exporting such commodities, which the foil or manusactures bring to persection. I shall not attempt tp enumerate the particular Iflands, but content myself with insorming you, they are found in greatest abundance in the West Indies; many of which are fo small, as to be the private property of a sew perfons.

Lady *Mary.* I never knew before that England was au Ifland: and always thought every thing we ate, drank, or wore, was the produce of our own Country.

Mentoria. Your Ladyship was much mistaken; on the contrary, we are indebted to other Countries and and Na-

tions, sor many of the conveniencies of lile. India supplies us with Tea, Spices, Drugs, Rice, China, Muflin, Precious Stones, and various other Articles. The West Indies, with Sugar, Coffee, Rum, Tobacco, Chocolate, Mahogany, Spices, Drugs, &c. &c. Italy surnishes us with most of the Silks we wear; as mulberry-trees, (on the leaves of which, SilkWorms seed,) are the natural growth of the country, and are as common there, as the oak, elm, &c. are in England. The Silk comes over in its natural state, is afterwards dyed of various, colours, and manufactured into the disserent kinds of Silk and Sattin we wear. Spain and Portugal produce must of the Wines we drink. France affords us Brandy, Claret, and some other Wines, with many ornamental parts of dress and surniture. Norway is samous sor timber, of which ships and many other things are built. Russia, Dantzic, and most of the Northern countries abound with, animals of various kinds; some docile, others serocious, many of which are valuable on account of their skins; such as the surs of theErmine, (which is the skin of a little animal very much like a weazle, and is generally called Miniver) Sables, Squirrels, Bears, &c &c. It was wisely ordained by Providence to. surnilit furnish the inhabitants of the Northern regions with such ample provision for warm raiment, as the coldness of the climate indispeniLly requires. In England, there are quarries of Hone, and mines os lead, tin, and coals; alfo in disserent parts of the world, quarries of marble, and mines of gold, silver, precious stones, and iron, which, to enumerate, would carry me beyond my present purpofe. Lady *Louisa.* Pray, Mentoria, what is a Peninsula? Is it not fomething like an ifland? *Mentoria.* You are persectly right, my dear Lady Louisa. It is a tract of land almost encompassed with water. The French call it *presque isle,* which, in their language, fo clearly expresses the sense, it requires no explanation. The neck of land which prevents it from becoming an ifland, is called *ijlhmus.* It consists of a piece of land which usually runs between two seas, and joins a peninsula to

the continent. Lady *Louisa.* I believe the next thing you are to explain, is rivers: I think you need not give yourself the trouble, as we know what they are. *Mentoria.* You have undoubtedly seen the river Thames; but but I am certain you cannot trace the source from whence that and other rivers spring. Lady *Louisa,* Does it not begin at London, and end at Richmond, *Merit or itu* I thought that was your Ladyship's idea, which is a false one; as they usually proceed from a spring or sountain, and empty themselves into some sea. The sea constantly ebbs and flows, which constitutes what are called Tides; this flux and reflux, renders the water more wholesome and agreeable than lakes of stajnated water, which cannot lofe the impurity they contract. Vessels also, from all parts of the world, come up with the tide to the port of London, and as a natural consequence, are conveyed from thence by the return oi it.

The Thames is the most famous river in England; there are many other of less consequence, which I have not leisure to enumerate. I shall only particularize the sollowing: the river Avon, which has often been celebrated on account of the great poet, Shake spear, being bom at a place called Stratsord-upon-Avon. The rivers Isis and Cam, are also famed sor their vicinity to the two universities of Oxsord and Cambridge; it is almost needless to add, the latter latter derives its name from a bridge being built over the river Cam. I cannot conclude this converfation on rivers, without adding fome account of the Nile. As it scarcely ever rains in Egypt, the foil would be quite unsruitsul, if it were not for the falutary effects of this wondersul river. It begins to rise at the latter end of May, and continues to do fo till September or October, when there are channels cut to let it into the great canal which runs through Cairo, from whence it overflows the sields and gardens. This joysul event is announced by a public sestival, sire-works and every demonstration of joy. The mud which the stream of the Nile carries with it, manures the earth, and makes it sit to receive the different kinds ofgrain, which in a month or two after it is fown, yields an abundant harvest. The Nile is fo very benesicial to the Egyptians, it feems to have been designed by Providence as a fovereign remedy for ail their evils, as even the plague, (which visits them once in fix or seven years) a diforder of the most malignant and fatal tendency, yet when the Nile overflows, this heavy scourge ceases. The cause is evidently this, all contagious diforders arise from the vitiated state of the air in extreme drought and heat, which is allayed by inundations tions or resreshing showers, and diffuses health to the inhabitants of such unsavourable eliminates.

Lady *Mary.*

Pray was not the famous Cleopatra, queen of Egypt?

Mcntoria.

Yes, my dear, though I believe we must consider her character and conduct, under the head of Roman history, as it is so inseparably 'connected with that of Mark Antony. It may not be amiss to insorm you, the vagrants usually called gypsies are reckoned natives of Egypt When the Sultan Selimus conquered the Egyptians, in the year 1417, they resused allegiance to his laws, and retired into the xleserts, living only by thest and plunder; at length they were banished from Egypt, and agreed to disperse themselves in small parties into every country in the known world. The art of magic, in which these people were allowed to excel, gained them in that unenlightened and credulous age, the reputation of foretelling events by the course of the planets, and other mysterious means. This opinion is now wholly exploded, and could never gain belief, but in a country absorbed in the grossest idolatry. Those who believe and acknowledge die omnipotence omnipotence of God, can never suppofe any inferior power possesses fore-knowledge ot any event incident to human lise; as that alone belongs to:he Creator of the universe, in whofe hands are the issues ot lise and death! Lord *George.* I agree with you, my dear Madam, in thinking none but very weak people can believe such absurdities; but I will not interrupt you, as I suppofe, you will now tell us

what a Promontory is.

Mentoria. A Promontory is a hill or point of land, which stretches itself over the sea; and is often called a Cape.

Lady *Loui/u.* What is a Mountain, my good Mentoria? I know it is a very large thing. *Mentoria.* It is a vast mass of earth; and when in a less degree it is called a Hill. Wales abounds with mountains, on which the wild goats browse. The Alps are very high mountains, which separate Germany from Italy; there is a passage over them, though rather dangerous. The tops of these mountains are always covered with snow; notwithstanding in the valleys beneath, there is the sinest verdure. The Pyreneau E mountains mountains divide France from Spain. The burning mountains of Vesuvius and Ætna, are wondersul phenomena of nature. The volcano, called Mount Ætna, is in the Ifland of Sicily, in the Mediterranean Sea, under the government of the King of Naples. The eruption of sire which bursts from it, is called the Lava; the top of the mountain from whence it proceeds, is stiled the Crater, or bowl. There have been whole towns laid in ashes by the streams of sire and combustible matter, of which these mountains are compofed; as wherever they issue or flow, they cause certain destruction. Lord *George.*

I should like very much to see Mount Ætna, and suppofe I shall, when I make the Tour of Europe. Pray, Mentoria, what is the difference between a Rock and a Mountain? I think that is the next, and last branch you have' to explain.

Mentoria.

Rocks are formed of a substance proverbially hard; and the sursace rough and uneven. They are situated in and near the sea, and are often pernicious to mariners: as the calamity usually called shipwreck, is produced by the ship striking on a rock, which either dashes it to pieces, or casts it upon fome defolate Ifland.

The

The Baltic Sea abounds with rocks. Hence it is, the voyages to Norway, and Denmark, are more dangerous than any other; and consequently wrecks are

more frequent, in that, than in any other Sea. There ate rocks in the Straits of Mesfina, called Scylla, and Charybdis, which are situated so critically, and the pasfage between them so narrow, that, whilst the mariners are striving to avoid one, they frequently split on the other.

Lady *Mary.*

Have you quite finished, my dear Mentoria? *Mentoria.*

For the present, my dear, having drawn you a rough sketch of the different parts of a map, which, I hope, will serve to impress my instructions on your mind; as you will find the subject I have just treated on, sully explained, in Plate I.

Es DIALOGUE V.

FRIDAY.

On the Derivation of Words, and Geography.

Lady *Mary.*

I Do not mean, my good Mentoria, to prescribe the subject of your instructions; yet I was so much pleased with the derivation of the word *Cambridge,* I wish you could recollect any instance of the fame nature. *Mentoria.* I will readily comply with your request, my dear Lady Mary; and though the instances I may produce, will not perhaps answer so literally, their reserence will be equally just, to some csrE 3 cumflance cumstance or word, in a soreign language; which expresses the sense, and constitutes the meaning. For example: the word *quadrupeds,* which signifies a sour-footed animal, is derived from the Latin, and literally means *Jour feet.* The *Adelphi* was called by that name, because it was built by brothers, which in Greek is expressed by the word *adelphos. Virginia* was discovered by Sir *Walter Raleigh,* in the reign of Queen *Elizabeth,* and called so, as a compliment to her, as she was never married.

Lady *Louisa.*

I hope, my dear Mentoria, you will point out some more examples; as I am much pleased with thofe you have produced. *Mentoria. Philadelphia,* a settlement in America, which is chiesly inhabited by Quakers, took its name from the particular tenets of that sect; which are a system of philanthropy and brotherly lov«. (Though I am no Grecian) I presume, the word *Philadelphia* is derived from the Greek, and means *brotherly love,* from *gihza to love,* and *afiKzo; a brother.* The *Cape of Good Hope* was discovered by the French, in endeavouring to find the NorthWest passage, which afforded them resreshment, metis, and inspired them with the *hope* of making other usesul discoveries: hence they called it The *Cape dt bonne Esperance.* Lord *George.* I wish you could tell the cause, from whence every thing takes its name. *Mentoria.* I shall now insorm you, from whence that Quarter of the world, called *America,* derives its origin. This vast tract of land was discovered by Christopher Columbus, a native of Genoa. Affairs of such great importance cannot always be completed by the projector: hence it was, that Americus Vefputius, a Florentine, immortalized his name by completing the work Columbus began, who undoubtedly had the greatest merit: notwithstanding, the whole country derived its name from *Americus Vefputius;* and as names of places are usually feminine, it was called *America.* Lady *Mary.* I think that was extremely unjust: I should think it very hard, if my sister did a sew leaves in my flower-piece, to have it called her basket of flowers. *Mentoria.* If we serioufly consider, Columbus does not seem in such a pitiable, nor Americus VespuE 4 this tius in such an enviable state, as at sirst fight we are apt to imagine. All persons of fense aml learning ascribe the merit to Columbus j whilst Vesputius, who arrogantly thought to engrofs the whole honour of the discovery, is difappointed, by (I venture to pronounce) half the world's not knowing from what, or whom, America took its name. I shall now subjoin a few observations on Geography; which, I hope, will entertain and improve you. Lord *George.* I am extremely glad, as it is a subject, which deeply engages my attention. *Mentoria.* I have already told you, the world is round: it is necessary, you mould know it is convex. Lady *Louisa.*

Pray, what is *convex,* my dear Mentoria? *Mentoria.* Convex is directly opposite to *concave.* To familiarize the idea: the outside of a tea-cup is *convex,* and the inside *concave.* I shall now insorm you, the top of the sphere or globe is called the Zenith: hence it is, this term is often used in a figurative sense, to describe a person in the most exalted state, by faying, they are in the zenith of their glory. The bottom of the the globe is called the Nadir: I thought I might, with equal propriety, use this term to express a state of depression, directly oppofite to the elevated situation, the word *Zenith* denotes; which I did in the following lines, though I can produce no authority for it.

The fame when in the Zenith of thy state,
Or in the Nadir of afflictive fate!

Lady *Mary.*

I never heard of these things before: pray, Mentoria, where did you get your knowledge? *Mentoria,* I am not conscious of possessing any extraordinary degree of knowledge: what I have attained, was by industry and observation. I have read a great deal, and was always desirous to keep company with perfons older than myself. The deserence I had for their judgment, which I knew was the result of long experience, induced me to follow their advice: hence it was, I escaped many errors, and was enabled to form my sentiments by the rules of prudence and discretion. I shall now explain to you, what the Antipodes are.

E5 Ladv

Lady *Louisa.* I cannot imagine what they can be: I never heard of them. - *Mentoria.* They are thofe perfons, who inhabit parts of the globe directly opposite to each other: consequently, as the world is round, the feet of the one must be directly parallel with the seet of the other. You will, I dare fay, sigure to yourself, that the antipodes walk on their heads, whilst you securely tread on your feet! Lord *George.* How, my good Mentoria, can it be otherwise? If a fly were to settle on the top of my cricket-

ball, and another at the bottom, would not the latter seem to walk on his head? *Mentoria.* Undoubtedly; but the world moves on an axis, and (if I may be allowed the expression) is air-hung: the space, in which it is suspended is called the horizon. Lord *George.* Pray, Mentoria, what is an Ais? *Mentoria.* As your Lordship compares the world to a cricket-ball, I shall pursue the simile. If you were to thrust a stick through the center of your your ball, which would enable you to turn it round, the stick, on which it moved, would be the axis.

Lady *Mary.* Is it past a doubt then, that the world moves? I am surprized, we do not perceive it. *Mentona.* There is not the least reason to question it. Hence it is, that we are the antipodes to thofe, who possess the opposite part of the globe. Our advantages are equal, though we enjoy them at different times. It is midnight with them, when it is noon-day with us. Their longest day is our shortest; and the length of their day is equal to the length of our night. The term *antipodes* is often used metaphors cally, to describe thofe persons, whofe sentiments and manners are diametrically opposite. Lady *Louisa.* I can scarcely believe, the world is in perpetual motion. *Mentoria.* The revolution of the earth on its own axis, is called the *diurnal* motion, which is persormed in the space of twenty-sour hours, and causes the succession of day and night. That part of the earth, which in the regular course E 6 is is hid from the light of the sun, must naturally fee involved in darkness; which constitutes what is called night: whilst the opposite part of the globe is cheered by the rays of the fun, and enjoys day-light with all its attendant comforts.

Iady *Alary.*

I understand this very clearly: but what causes morning and evening? *Mentoria.*

The oblique direction of the rays of the sun, which are produced by the regular gradation of the earth, in her process round the sphere, in which she moves.

Lady *Louisa.*

Pray, my dear Mentoria, do not clofe this entertaining subject so soon. *Mentoria.*

It is not my intent, my dear Lady Louifa. I shall now proceed to explain, what causes the vicissitude of heat and cold, and the regular succession of the seasons. The earth, as a planet, performs its course round the sun in three hundred and sixty-five days, which is called a solar year. Heat is occasioned by the rays of the sun being transmitted in a perpendicular direction and cold from the cesfation, or or obliquity of its rays. The difserent seasons are produced, as a natural consequence, by our being near, or distant from the sun; which makes us seel its power, in a greater or less degree. The gradual change from one season to another, is produced by the regular process of the earth's revolution round the sun. I shall now proceed to explain the difserent climates, which are classed under the title of Zones.

Lady *Mar-y.*

I think, I have read of people wearing zones; so that it appears not probable, any part of dress can have the least connection with Geography.

Mentoria.

Zone signifies a girdle, or any thing which" encompasses: hence it is, these divisions of the earth are called so, because they go round the globe. There are five zones; one *torrid* which is a term sor extreme heat; as the fun is vertical, or directly over the head twice every year, and also produces no shadow: this climate is intensely hot. The countries, situated under the torrid zone, are the Continent of Africa, Guinea, Lybia, Abyssinia, Arabia Felix, East India, some part of America. rica, and New Guinea, with many iflands, the inhabitants of which are chiefly black. Lady *Louisa.*

I should not like to live under the torrid zone; should you, Mentoria? *Mentoria.* Certainly none would choofe a situation, where the difadvantages are fo evident. We are now going to consider the two *temperate* zones (under one of which, we are fo fortunate to be placed.) They are called fo, from being situated

between the torrid and frigid zones; and are distinguished by the Northern temperate zone, and the Southern temperate zone. Under the former England is situated, Spain, France, Germany, Italy, Scotland, Ireland, the greatest part of Norway, Sweden, Denmark, Poland, Russia, the Lesser Asia, Natolia, Greece, Judea or Palestine, Assyria, and the chief part of the Greater Asia, viz. Armenia, Persia, part of India, of great Tartary, and of China, Japan, and the chief part of North America, with many i stands. Under the South temperate zone lie the uttermost part of Africa, and the Cape of Good Hope;. as alfo a great part of South America. Lady *Mary.*

I suppofe, we shall now hear about the frigid zones, which you just now mentioned.

Mentoria, Mentoria.

The two *frigid* zones derive their name, from their situation being intensely cold. Under the North frozen zone, Greenland and Spitsbergen are situated, famous for the whalesishery; with the greatest part of Tartary, the points of Norway and Swedeland, the heart of Lapland and Finland, the uttermost part of America, and the bounds of Europe. The boisterous winds, and rough seas, prevent the countries being well known, that He under the South irozen zone. There have been many attempts made, which have hitherto proved unsuccesssul, on account of the sickness, want of provisions, and other hardsiiips the failors must undergo in such a severe climate; which discourages them from making surther discoveries.

Lord *George.*

If you were compelled to live under one of the zones, vyhich would you preser, the frigid or torrid?

Mentoria.

I will leave it to your own judgment, when I have explained the advantages and difadvantages incident to each. Providence has wisely ordained, that in thofe climates, where the heat heat difables the inhabitants from severe labour, there is an abundance of all the productions of the earth; and has granted the blessing of plenty, to compenfate for the

want of health, and other comforts their situation deprives them of. Riches seem indispenfably necessary to thofe, who inhabit any hot country, as they not only minister the conveniences, but the luxuries of lise, which, in fome degree, are necessary to alleviate the lassitude and inactivity the climate produces. Lady *Louisa.*

I have not the least doubt, I should prefer the torrid to the frigid zone. *Mentoria.*

Be not hasty in your determination; always, hear both sides of the question, belore you determine in favour of either. I am inclined to thfifrk, I shou!d stand neuter; though I do not mean to bias your judgment. Lady *Mary.*

Now, my dear Mentoria, point out the advantages of the frigid zone: the profpect appears fo very dreary, I cannot imagine in what they consist.

Mentoria.

The coldness of the climate renders the foil unfruitsul, in all vegetable productions. To compensate compenfate for this desiciency, thofe countries abound with animals of different kinds, which afford food and raiment; alfo sish of various forts. The inhabitants are very industrious, and can endure insinite fatigue: all the comforts they enjoy, are produced by their own labour: neither can there be a stronger-incitement to industry, than the reflection, that our sustenance depends upon the full exertion of our abilities. A sincere endeavour to produce this effect, is ever blessed with means, by the kind hand of Providence. In many of the remote countries of the frozen zone, there are no means of obtaining food, but by hunting or sishing, as there is no refource of a market. Neither can the inhabitants fay, " To day I "will have veal for dinner; I am tired of "mutton;" as Providence, not choice, surnishes their repast, and which, from the share of health and strength they enjoy, is often better relished than all the Asiatic dainties. They are usually long-lived, which may be accounted for thus: as heat causes an univerfal lassitude, by relaxing the nervous system, and consequently shortens the duration of lise; fo it follows, as a natural consequence, that cold braces up and invigorates the human frame, which which produces many instances of longevity. Every situation in lise has its peculiar advantages. As every blessing we enjoy, lofes part of its value by possession, I am clearly of opinion, thofe circumstances, which appear to us in a formidable light, are not esteemed such great evils by thofe accustomed to their pressure. There is a passage in Pope's Essay on Man, which, by taking the liberty to alter one word, is applicable to my present purpofe.

But where th' extreme of cold was ne'er agreed, Ask where's the North? At York, 'tis on the

Tweed; In Scotland at the Orcades, and there At Greenland, Zembla, or the Lord knows where. No creature owns it in the sirst degree, But thinks his neighbour surther gone than he: Ev'n those, who dwell beneath its very zone, Or never seel the rage, or never own. What happier natures shrink at with affright, The hard inhabitant contends is right.

Lady *Louisa*. I still think, I had rather live where there was great plenty and elegance, than be subject-to such difficulties.

Mentoria. Mentoria.

What, my dear, would it avail you, to have your table surnished with all the luxuries the East could asford, if you were not blessed with an appetite to relish them? Your situation would be similar to that of Tantalus, who had always delicious fruits and water before his eyes, though he was never able to taste either; which was inslicted on him, as an heavy punishment.

Lady *Mary*.

But if we lived in thofe countries, we should have flaves to carry us about on palanquins, with canopies over our heads, and attendants to fan us.

Mentoria.

I have fo good an opinion of your Ladyship's disposition, as to think, when you viewed this circumstance in a serious light, it would give you great pain; as nothing can more deeply affect an ingenuous mind, than seeing a sellow-creature reduced to the necessity of suffering any hardships, we cannot endure

ourselves; which is greatly increased, when we reflect, our convenience is the cause. I can scarcely imagine, the human heart can be fo callous in the seelings of philanthropy, as ever wholly wholly to be divested of pity and compassion; and am inclined to believe, sor the honour of the human species, they are often stifled, though but seldom extinguished.

The human mind, with sense of pity wrought,
Yields to the force of sympathetic thought;
Form'd of a texture, which no eye can trace,
Folly, and guilt, its brightness does efface:
Apt to receive impressions, nor retain Thofe, which review'd, cause sear and endless
pain. As notes of music, bending to the touch, Produce harsh discord, if they're press'd to« much; Yet, if the whole in sull accordance join, The mental harmony is then divine!

Lady *Louisa*. I am quite of your opinion, my dear Mentoria, and think I should never take long journeys, if they were persormed by such painsul means; as every step the flaves took, would make me uneasy.

Mentoria. We shall find in this, as in most other instances of lise, the less we depend on others, the the better the different sunctions of our state are persormed. Providence has endued us with the faculties of motion, and granted us organs suited to the purpose; the sull exertion of which is more agreeable and conducive to health, than any vehicle luxury or art can invent; though, under many circumstances, they are extremely usesul.

Lady *Mary*. What state then, my good Mentoria, do you preser?

Mentoria. Without doubt, that which is exempt from the rigor of the frigid zone, and the sultry heat of the torrid. Such is the happy predicament, in which we stand; as our country is under the temperate zone. The agreeable vicissitude of the seafons, and the abundance we enjoy, should inspire our hearts with gratitude, for such inestimable blessin-

gs, denied to fo great a part of the human species. Our land is not scorched, by being situated under the meridian of the sun; neither are our seas frozen, by being deprived of his cheering power: his radiant beams are dispensed in such just proportion to our wants, as to produce all the comforts and conveniences of life. There is another peculiar peculiar advantage in our situation, that our manners preseive the medium between the Northern barbarity, and Eastern luxury; and form a system of politeness and urbanity, which is ever acceptable and engaging. Lady *Louisa*.

I now rejoice in the comforts of our situation, and should be forry to change it for any other. But is this all, my dear Mentoria, you intend to fay on the subject?

Mentoria.

I shall endeavour to form a metaphorical allusion of the degree of comparifon the different climates will bear to the difserent states of lise; and shall begin this enquiry, by comparing grandeur and power to the torrid zone; not only from the luxury whicn attends it, but alfo because they oppress thofe, who seel their weight. The flaves, who are licensed in thofe countries, are like the venal flatterers, who are subservient to thofe in power, and whofe freedom is bartered for gain. Lady *Mary*.

What is the next point, you intend to explain?

Mentoria.

The similitude between the temperate zones, and the state of lise usually called competency: they they both afford every requisite necessary to our happiness. Riches, as well as heat, in the superlative degree, are in general oppressive to the possessors, and rather cause pain than pleasure, from their attendant consequences. On the contrary, moderate wealth, like a tern, perate clime, makes every object smile with peace and plenty.

Lady *Louisa*. My dear Mentoria, are you not now draw, ing a comparison, from the state of lise we are in?

Mentoria. Yes, my dear; and am going to trace that, from which you are happily exempt. The traits are so strong, which sorm the likeness of poverty to the frigid zone, they are easily delineated. It is needless to insorm you, this state deprives all, who are under its dominion, of every source of sustenance or support, but 'what is.obtained by the efforts of their own industry. As the seas of the frigid zone are sometimes frozen, and resuse their produce to the inhabitants of thofe parts; so too often is the human heart petrified, and incapable of receiving the soft impression of pity; and the tears congealed, which ought to flow in commiseration miseration of the indigent. Health and strength are annexed to both these states, which arise from the fame cause, a total exemption from inactivity and luxury.

Lady *Mary.*

But are these people happy, my dear Mentoria?

Mentoria.

The beautisul lines, I have just recited from Pope, clearly indicate, the inhabitants of the frigid zone are not dissatisfied with their situation. It appears equally clear to me, that poverty is not incompatible with happiness; as by industry all the necessaries of lise may be acquired, which are all our state requires. These, with temperance and health, place thofe who possess them above contempt, though they are entitled to our compassion and assistance.

Lady *Louisa.*

What a striking resemblance you have pointed out, which I should never have thought of! What effect ought it to have on my mind? *Mentoria.*

If you apply it to your own situation, you are to inser from thence, that the state which is allotted you, in respect of climate and station of of lise, is a peculiar blessing. It will alfo teach you not to envy the powersul, nor despise the indigent; the former being only entitled to respect, the latter to your best endeavours to relieve their distresses; as the true use of riches consists in supplying our own wants, which should ever be consined within the rules of temperance and frugality, that we may be enabled to provide for the necessities of others.

DIALOGUE VI, SATURDAY.

On History; with the Life of Romulus and Remus.

Mentoria.

I Propofe, my dears, this morning, to give you a short dissertation on history; and shall endeavour to convince you of the necessity ot your making it your peculiar study. Lady *Mary.* Are there not many different kinds of history, my dear Mentoria?

Mentoria. Undoubtedly my dear. I will proceed to consider them under their different classes, and shall begin with the scriptures, which are often called *sacred hijlory*; to which I shall oppofe the heathen mythology, which contains a deF 2 scription scription of the deities worshipped by the heathens; from hence called *profane history.*Lady *Louisa.* What history do you think is most proper for us to read? *Mentoria.* I shall pursue the discussion of each particular branch, and then determine my choice. *Natural hijlory* delineates all the productions of nature, and enables us to form an idea of all her works: such as animals, silhes, birds, infects, trees, plants, ores, fossils, &c. &c. *Biography,* or the history of famous, perfons, is very entertaining, and aWo instructive, as it inspires the mind with a desire to attain those qualities, which have fo eminently distinguished others. The history of your own countrv teaches you the progress of arts, manufactures, and commerce, and clearly proves the advantages which are derived from a well regulated state; is alfo insorms you of the various means which were used to form the system os the British constitution. The persecution and arbitrary measures authorized in former times, should excite in us joy and gratitude, for the lenity and freedom of the present go;, vernment. Ancient history, (particularly the Roman) enlarges the understanding, and qualisies fies us sor the perufal of polite authors, as it is necessary to be acquainted with the manners os the ancients, in order to sorm a competent knowledge of those of the moderns. Lord *George.* Was not Rome once a very famous place; and inhabited by persons of extraordinary sense and learning? *Mentoria.* It was the seat of Empire, as well as of polite arts and literature, notwithstanding which, the luxury and esseminacy that prevailed, subverted the government; and at present it is only lamed, by being the Papal See, and consequently the residence of the Pope, Cardinals, &c. and also sor ths magnificence of the buildings, fine paintings, ruins, &c.

Lady *Mary,* 'Now, rny good Mentoria, will you tell us which history is the most proper for us to read?

Mentoria. My dear Lady Mary, in order to silence your importunate entreaties, I must declare it is absolutely necessary you should be well read in all. At present, I wish facred and natural history to be the chief objects of your attention; as they both tend to increase your love F 3 and and admiration of the deity. When you are a little farther advanced in lise, I shall recommend to your perusal the history of England, and a'so that of the Romans. In this course of reading, you will meet with a number of entertaining anecdotes and surprizing circumstances, which attended the lives of famous persons, whom you now only know by name. History will introduce you to a farther acquaintance with them, and enable you very soon to give as clear an account of Cato, Demosthenes, Mark Antony, &c. as if you were personally acquainted with them. Lady *Mary.*

From whence did Rome derive its name?

Mentoria. From Romulus, who built the city. I should imagine it would be agreeable to you, to know some particulars of the sounder of so great a capital. 1 shall therefore give you a sketch os his character, and that of his brother Remus, as they are drawn by Plutarch the samous biographer.

Lady *Louisa.* Is his lise entertaining, my dear Mentoria? if it be, I shall attend to it with pleasure. *Mentoria.* I think it is remarkably so, my dear Lady Louifa, which made me choofe to recite it.

The *t*

The Life of ROMULUS and REMUS.

THE kings of Alba being lineally descended from Æneas, the succession devolved upon Numitor and Amulius, who were brothers. In order amicably' to settle the division of the. empire, the treasures, which were brought from Troy, were placed on one fide, and the kingdom on the other. Numitor chofe the kingdom, consequently the riches were the possession of his brother. Amulius soon dethroned Numitor; and, searing his daughter might have children, who would lay claim to the crown, he made her a priestess of the goddess Vesta, to prevent her entering into the marriage state, as none but single women were admitted of that order. This lady, whofe name was Rhea Sylvia, being not suited to the office appointed her, was. soon discovered to be pregnant, for which fte was sentenced to undergo a severe punishment; but Antho, the daughter of Amulius, espoused her cause, and prevailed on her father to change her punishment into confinement and solitude. In this retirement, she was delivered of two sons, remarkable sor their size and beauty, F 4 which »' which created jealousy in the tyrant's breast, and induced him to form plans for their destruction: to effect: which, he commanded a servant to destroy them. Tlie person who undertook to perform this horrid deed, put the children into a trough, and carried them to the banks of a river, with intent to cast them in; but the water being unusually rough and high, the sear of endangering his own fafety, induced him to leave the trough on the shore, and make a precipitate retreat. The high tide of the river bore it up,, and conveyed it to an even shore, near which there stood a sig tree, which sheltered the children from the rays of the sun: it is also faid a she wolf suckled them, and a wood-pecker brought them their daily sood. They were discovered in this situation by Faustulus, herdsman to Amulius, who brought them to his wise, from whom they received every attention their helpless state required. As they advanced in lise, they were distinguished by their strength, courage, aud greatness of soul. Remus was of an active turn of mifid, and of an enterprizing spirit. Romulus was of a different disposition, inclined to study, and naturally prudent. .They signalized themselves in a quarrel which happened between the herdsmen of Nuruitoi and and Amulius, which maniested their merit, and divulged the mystery ot' their birth. Romulus and Remus oppofed the herdsmen of Numitor, as they thought them to be the aggressors. They alfo associated with thofe perfons, who, either from their poverty or being in the bonds of ilavery, wished to effect a revolution in the-state. Lord *George.* Were they not very much to blame, to keep company with such perfons, and take part against their grand-father? *Mentoria.* Nothing can excuse the former, except the supposition, that they groaned under oppression, and naturally wished to obtain their freedom, or fome other advantage equally necessary to their happiness r the latter charge is wholly extenuated, by their total ignorance of their parentage and noble descent. To pursue the history, every thing was ripe for a rebellion; when Remus was taken prifoner, whilst Romulus was facriftcing to the gods. He was carried before his grandfather Numitor, and charged with several crimes, who reserred him to Amulius to receive sentence. After having demanded fatisfaction for the injuries his ser-' vants had sustained, Amulius sent him to Numitor, to receive sentence adequate to the ofF 5 fence since he was guilty of. Numitor, so far from inslicting one that was severe, ordered him to his own house; as during the examination, he perceived something in his countenance which deeply engaged his attention, and induced him to make enquiries respecting his descent and way os lise. To which Remus returned this spirited reply:

"Your justice in examining, besore you "condemn, deserves, on my part, the return "of truth and sincerity. I am a stranger to "my family and descent; I have but one "twin brother; we have ever been considered "as the sons of a shepherd; but since our ac"dilation, it has been rumoured we are of "noble extraction. Our birth is mysterious; "our support in insancy miraculous; as a she "wolf suckled us, and a wood-pecker supplied "us with nourishment, whilst we lay in a neg"lected and helpless state by a river's side. "The'trough is preserved which contained us, "and the inscription still legible: these, per"haps, may be discovered by our unhappy "parents, when we are no more!"

Numitor was much affected with this speech, the young man's appearance, and the substance of his narration, agreeing with the time his daughter's children were born, induced him to hope hope they were her descendants: to confirm which, he had an interview with his daughter, who was then in prison. Faustulus, the herdsman, thought in this critical juncture of affairs, any surther cklay would be dangerous, so he insormed Romulus of his real birth, and resolved to produce the trough, as a testimony of the real parentage of these young men. ' Lady *Mary.*

You cannot imagine, my dear Mentoria, how much I seel myself interested in their history!
Mentoria.
Faustulus was at length determined to carry the trough to Numitor; his apparent haste and anxiety, betrayed the importance of his errand. Unsortunately, one of the guards who observed his eagerness, and was present when the children were left on the shore, and recollecting the trough and inscription, immediately insormed Amulius of his discovery; who behaved as persons usually do that are enraged, and in fear of being detected in a bad action. He dispatched a messenger to Numitor, to enquire if his daughter's children were alive who, finding Numitor inclined to, acknowledge the young men to be his. grandchildren, adviled him to assert his right, and offered to F 6 affi.st assist him in fo arduous an undertaking. Thing were now brought to a crisis. Romulus appearing at the head of a numerous band ot hiscompanions; the citizens from the hate they bore to the usurper, readily revolted. Thusby commanding a powersul army, and Remus previoufly having gained the populace over to his-cause,' Arnulius wa&dethroned, and being unabled to make asnjP resistance or toescxpe, he was seized andpвнo death. The two brothers were now in possession of the kingdom of Alba, but did not choofe to reside there, without hold-

ing the reins of government, which they could not do consistent with, equity, as it was their grand-father's inheritance. After having resigned the kingdom to Numitor, and with silial piety discharged their duty to their mother, they formed a pianos living together, and determined to build a city amongst the Hills, where they received their education. In order to increase the number of their subjects, they caused their territoriesto be a resuge for all who had violated the laws of their own country, and dreaded the punishment due to their crimes. These considerations foon placed our heroes at the head of a numerous army. They now differed respecting the place where the city was to be built.

built. Romulus wished it to be built where hehad made a square of houses, which he called Rome; but Remus thought the Aventine Mount a more eligible situation: at length they agreed it should be determined by Augury, or the flight of birds. The divination proved in favour os Romulus, as twelve vultures appeared,to In:::, whilst Remus, faw but half the number.

Wry *Louisa*

How very finlSh it was to let the flight of birds determine such an important affair! *Menttria.*

Your astonishment, my dear, will cease, when you reflect, that he Pagans were guided inall their actions; by means equally delusive: such as the *oracles,* which were sentiments delivered in so mysterious and ingenious a manner, as to bear any construction that suited' their purpose; or by the flight of birds, blood, of animals, &c. some of which were thought a good omen, and others portentous of some heavy calamity. There cannot possibly be a 'stronger argument, to prove that every creature is inclined to worfliip, and seek the aid os a superior power, as in thofe early times, when the gospel was not revealed, and the greatest part of the world were totally ignorant ot the ex» istence jslencc and power of the great Creator, they sought redress from, and implored the assistance of the sun, moon, stars, birds, beasts, statues, &x.

to which they ascribed the power of relieving their necessities. We must now return to Romulus, who, as soon as he had gained his point, began to put his plan in execution. Remus affected to despise his brother's attempt to sortify the city. and. whilst the soundation of the wall was dig BBg, with a degree of insolent contempt, leaped over the ditch; which enraged Romulus so much, it is faid he killed him on the spot. Faustulus, the good old herdsman, was also stain in the scuffle. Romulus buried his brother, and old friend, with great pomp and solemnity, and then proceeded to build the city. Lady *Mary.*

What an act of cruelty it was in Romulus to murder his brother, sor so flight an offence, which at most deserved but a trifling reprimand! I think he must be very unhappy afterwards. *Mentoria.*

I dare fay it gave him but little, or perhaps n o uneasiness; as in thofe days it was not thought such a heinous offence sor any person to take away either their own lise, or that of another, there being then no distinction between rashness and and courage; and such acts of violence and cruelty, were more srequently applauded ihan condemned. Lord *George.*

I want very much to hear how he went on with the city. *Mentoria.*

Previous to laying the foundation, he sent to Tuscany for workmen to direct the forms and ceremonies due on such occasions. They began by digging a trench»round the building, designed for the court of justice; into which they threw the sirst fruits of all valuable productions'both, of art and nature. Each os them alfo, took a small portion of the foil of the country from whence thev came, and cast it in promiscuoufly. This trench was to form the centre of the city, round which they were to mark the distance for the extent.

The founder, seated on a brazen plough-share, yoked together a bull and a cow, and turned a deep surrow round the bounds of the city. He lifted up the plough, where he intended to place the gates, fo that they were a free pasfage

for things mystical or profane; notwithstanding every other part was held facred. This city was began on the 21st os April.

About 751 years before the birth of Christ.

The The anniverfary of this memorable event was a high sestival amongst the Romans. The citybeing complete, all who were able to bear arms, were enrolled into companies of three thoufand foot guards, and three hundred horse, which were called legions, as they were selected from the rest os the people. He alfo chose an hundred men of distinguished abilities for his counsellors, whom he called patricians, and the whole body the senate. To mark the different ranks of life, he fliled the semic the patrons, and tne populace or plebeians clients. The next point be considered was, the population of the city, as without women it would foon havt'been defolate. To effect this purpofe, he had recourse to the following stratagem: he caused it to be proclaimed, that the altar of a god had! been discovered under ground, and appointed a day for a folemn facrisice and public games. Most of the inhabitants, with their wives and daughters, came from the neighbouring villages to the celebration of this sestival. Romulus was clad in purple, and seated in the midst of his nobles. It was previoufly agreed to seize all the young women, when Romulus gave the sign or token, by rising from his seat, and throwinghis robe over his body. As foon as ke gave the signal, they drew their swords, and, 1 and, with a loud shout, seized the daughters of the Sabines, to the number of about 683. The Sabines were a numerous and warlike people, residing chiefly in small unsortisied villages. This injured nation sent ambasfadors to Romulus, to insist on their daughters being restored; and alfo to propofe forming an alliance on more equitable terms. Romulus rejected this proposition, though he wished to preserve their friendship.

Lady *Lauisa.*

My dear Mentoria, I sincerely pity the Sabine women for being taken from their friends: how hard I should think it to be torn from tny parents! Was it not very cruel of Romulus to seize them? *Mentoria.*

Nothing can be urged in his desence, except the exigence of his situation. There are some instances, in which acts ot oppression are sheltered under the term os state policy, and stand exempt from reproach, on account of the good effects they produce. Lord *George.*

I am surprized the Sabines did not resist the power of Romulus. *Mentoria.*

We are now come to the part of the history, which insorms us, Acron the king of the Ceninensians attacked this new settlement. Romulus was not prepared to desend himself, by any other means than single combat, in which he came off victorious, he killed Acron, routed bis army, and took possession of the capital. This event did not discourage the Sabines from profecuting their intended war; ac-. cordingly they chofe Tatius for their general, who marched against Rome. The citadel was well fortisied, and commanded by Tarpeius, a man of great valour; his daughter, Tarpeia, instigated by love or avarice, betrayed one of the gates to the Sabines: she claimed as her reward, all they wore on their left arms, which consisted of a golden bracelet and buckler. This traitress met with the punishment her crime deserved, for as Tatius, the general of the Sabines threw his buckler at her, the whole army following his example, fire was crushed to death.

The battle was carried on a long time, with great flaughter on both sides; but was interrupted by the interposition of the Sabine women, who were settled in Rome. Their frantic cries, when they beheld the dead bodies of their husbands and fathers, caused a scene of general consusion. The two armies sell back to hear hear their complaints and expostulations, which were to this effect: "What crimes have we "committed to deserve such reueated and un"merited misfortunes. We were rmde wives by "compulsion, though duty has at length indu"ced us to love those whom at sirst we regard"ed with horror and detestation. Do not, from "the idea of redressing the grievances we "have sustained,

separate us from our hus"bands and children; and notwithstanding "you may have other motives for engaging in "this war, we hope, for our fakes, you will "cease hostilities. We behold our kindred "every where, resign us therefore to our hus"bands and children, as the being separated "from them would be the worst captivity we "could experience!

Their entreaties had the desired effect, and produced a treaty of peace. This act of heroism, caused an edict to be made in favour of the Roman women, to exempt them from all labour but spinning. The Romans and Sabines were to inhabit the city on equal terms. It was agreed the city should be called Rome, from Romulus; but the inhabitants Quirites, from Cures, the capital of the Sabines. The power of the two kings was to be equal.

This This form of government continued in an uninterrupted flate of harmony sor five years, but was disturbed by the sollowing circumstance i. the friends of Tatius happened to meet some ambafadors who were going to Rome, whom they robbed and murdered. Romulus was of opinion this crime deserved immediate punishment, but his colleague oppofed this measure, as he feared the being deprived of thofe men would weaken his power. The relations of the ambassadors, sought an opportunity to be revenged on Tatius, and effected their purpose by seizing him at a village near Rome, where, with Romulus, he was offering a facrifice, and he sell a victim to their resentment.

The Veientes declared war against Romulus, by remanding the' city of Fidenæ, which he had taken; but their army was defeated, and a truce made sor an hundred years. This was the last war in which Romulus engaged. Lord *George.*

The affairs of Romulus now seem to bear a very favourable aspect, as he appears to have subdued his enemies, and to be in possession of the kingdom without a rival.

Mentoria. These flattering views proved but of a very short short duration; and vanished almost as foon as they ap-

peared. Elated with his profperity, he grew imperious and assuming. The complacency and condescension which rendered him fo amiable, were now obscured by pride and petulance. He clothed himsels in a purple vest, over which he wore a loofe robe with a purple border; and received thofe who were admitted into his presence on a chair of state, with every appendage of magnisicence and royalty.

He was attended wherever he went, by several lictors, or executioners, each bearing art ax bound up with a bundle of rods, to denote their power to punish. This conduct of Romulus met with universal difapprobation. The senators were more particularly his enemies, on account of the little attention he paid to their counsels. In order to revenge the insults they sustained, they formed a plan to seize him, whilst he was holding an assembly in the temple of Vulcan; which they effected by cutting him in pieces, and each taking away part of his body, they caused it to be proclaimed, he was carried up to heaven in a whirlwind. This account did not gain belief; consequently the people people were inclined to make surther enquiries, respecting the death of their king.

Whilst this sedition was in its insancy, Julius Proculus, a man of unblemished character, folemnly depofed, that as he was travelling on the road, he met Romulus arrayed in bright armour, with a divine aspect; who thus addressed him:

"It has been ordained by the gods, O Pro' culus, that I should return to heaven, from "whence I came, aster having built a city, and "formed a system of government, which will "be an example for suture ages. Insorm the "Romans, that, by the exercise of manly vir"tues, they will attain the height of human "glory; and alfo that their king, transformed "into the god Quirinus, will grant all their "petitions. Fare ye well." Lady *Mary.*

Did the Romans believe this pretended vision? *Menioria.*

It gained univerfal belief; which is not to be wondered at in such a superstitious age: they alfo worshipped him, as their tutelar Deity. Thus did Romulus fall, in the sifty-fourth year of of his age, and thirty-eighth of his reign; a striking instance, how very sew are proof against the allurements of magnificence, and a series of prosperity. He was punctual in the performance of all religious rites and ceremonies, and generally carried the crooked rod in his hand, used by magicians to mark out the heavens. He also pretended to be deeply skilled in the occult sciences. His wisdom was manisested by the laws he instituted, amongst which he specified no punishment sor parricide; as he suppofed, no human creature could be so abandoned, as to commit it: nor was there ever an instance known, till fix hundred years after. The unsavourable circumstances, which attended the final scene of the lise of Romulus, were the natural consequence of his arbitrary proceedings, and his unbounded passion sor power and glory; desires, which, if they are not restrained by prudence and humanity, are ever destructive in their consequence.

Lady *Louisa.*

I am sorry, dear Mentoria, this entertaining History is finished: I like it almost as well as the Fairy Tales.

Men to ri.

I am glad you are pleased with it, my dear Lady Louifa: you must treat part of it as a fable, *y* sable, and only take the facts which are recited, in a literal sense.

»' Lady *Mary.*

Pray, my dear Madam, what is *parricide,* I suppose it is a very great crime.

Mentoria. It is the most heinous offence that can be committed, as it consists of the murder of a father. Matricide is the term to express the murder of a mother; fratricide of a brother; regicide of a king; homicide of a man; suicide of one's self: hence it is the Jews are called *decides,* because they murdered Christ, who 'was the son of God.

Lady *Louisa.* What is the Tutelar Deity, my good Mentoria?

Mentoria. The term *tutelar* signifies a guardian or protector. Minors who are under the direction of a guardian or tutor, are faid to be in a state of tutelage; there are tutelar faints as well as deities.

St. George is fliled the Saint of England, St. Andrew of Scotland, St. Patrick of Ireland, St. David of Wales, St. Lewis of France, St. Mark of Venice, besides manyothers. These were all persons who distinguished tinguished themselves by some heroic actions. The countries which derived the advantage, desirous of rendering their memory immortal, canonized them as saints; and appointed an annual sestival to commemorate their heroes, and celebrate them as the guardians and protectors of their country. i DIALOGUE VII. SUNDAY. On the Church-Service, with an Explanation of the Parable of Nathan and David.

Mentoria. LADIES, as *Sunday* is a day set apart for the worship of God, I shall prohibit all trifling pursuits, and endeavour to employ your time suitable to fo laudable a purpofe. Lady *Mary.* I should be forry to act contrary to the *cx*press commands of God, which enjoin us to keep holy the Sabbath Day, and to abstain from all kinds of work. But I wonder why we are G 2 forbidden forbidden to pursue our business on this day; as I cannot see any reason, it should be offensive to

God, for us to do our duty by working, &c.

Men ter ia.

To give you a clear idea of the institution of the Sabbath, it is necessary to insorm you,

the division of time, usually called a *week,* is a type or symbol of the creation of the world,

which is clearly explained in the sourth commandment: " For in six days the Lord made

"heaven and earth, the sea, and all that in

"them is; and rested the seventh day: where-

"fore the Lord blessed the seventh day, and

"hallowed it." In like manner, we persorm all that we have to do, in six days, and rest the seventh, in commemoration of the manisold blessings we receive at the hand of God. A

cessation from labour is necessary to effect this great purpofe; as the avocations

and pursuits,

in which the greatest part of the human species are employed, would not allow them sufficient time sor serious consideration, nor permit them regularly to attend divine service

Lady *Louisa.*

I always thought, my good Mentoria, Sunday was a day of rejoicing; as every body seems happy and cheersul. For my own part,

Hike *4.*

I like it better than any day in the week, because I get no task: yet you fay, if people worked, it would not allow time for serious consideration. I cannot see the reafon for being serious on a holiday. *Mentoria.* In this you are mistaken, my dear Lady Louifa; as the term *holiday,* like many others, is strangely degenerated, and perverted from the original intention. A moment's reflection will convince you of your error; as there requires no other conviction, but to divide the word into *holy-day,* which implies a day that is to be kept facred. Cheersulness is not prohibited: thofe, who conscientioufly discharge their duty, generally possess this quality in the greatest degree. It is the natural consequence of having acted agreeable to the rules of right reafon; as the self-approbation, which arises from, the persormance of religious rites, inspires the mind with that temper and conduct, which alone deserve the name os Cheersulness. Whilst, on the contrary, Levity (which the weak and inconsiderate mistake for Mirth) is incompatible with, the duty we owe to our Creator; as it obscures the only resemblance we can possibly bear to him, which consists ire. G 3. the the full exertion of our reafon, and mental faculties,

Lady *Mary.* I am quite ashamed, when I reflect how inattentive I have been on these occasions, which I now sind, required serious attention; but am refolved, nothing shall induce me to. commit the fame fault in suture.

Mentoria. That is all which will be required of you. The frailty of our nature subjects us to frequent mistakes, which are only sinsul, when we do not recover as fast as possible from our errors, nor avoid the repetition of thofe, which either our own experience, or the kind admonitions of our friends, have pointed out to us. Lady *Louisa*. I am sure, my dear Mentoria, I shall never again be careless and inattentive at church; but shall regard my duty, and serioufly listen to the minister, who persorms the service. *Mentoria*. This attention, my dear Lady Louifa, is abfolutely necessary. To convince you nothing can excuse the neglect of it, I shall insorm you, the Church-Service is divided into two parts, *supplication* and *thanksgiving*. Supplication is is the request and humble petitions offered at the Throne of Grace, for the continuation or increase of the comforts or conveniences of lise; or to be relieved from any trouble, which oppresses us, such as sickness, want, &c. There requires but little to be faid, in order to convince you, this part of the Service demands fervor and humility, to make our petitions acceptable. The absurdity of a contrary conduct cannot be more clearly evinced, than by supposing, you wished to procure any temporal advantage, to effect which you obtained an audience of an ejrthly potentate; it will not admit of a doubt, but that, when you were conducted into his presence, you would be inspired with a degree of awe, which would prevent any unguarded look or expression falling from you: neither, when you began to plead your cause, would you suffer your dress, or any external object, to divert vour alteration from the great end you had in view. If this conductis due to the creature, how can we raise our ideas sufsiciency high, to persorm acceptable service to the Creator? Our insinite obligations cannot be exceeded, but by his mercy, which.; is extended over all his works; for it is in Him aloae, we live, move, and have. our Lei:ig.

G 4 Lady

Lady *Mary*.

I am so thoroughly convinced of the necessity of paying the greatest attention to everything which is facred, that it will not only influence my conduct in the public worship of God, but also, for the suture, make me more devout when

I say my prayers in private. I will.not, roy dear Mentoria, interrupt you any longer; as I am impatient to hear your definition of thanksgiving.

Mentoria. Thanksgiving is the gratesul sense we seel, for any favour or benesit received; which is. testified by acknowledging, in the most public and solemn manner, the obligations we owe to our benesactors. Thofe, which we receive at the hand of God, bear no degree of comparison, with any that can be derived from a prince or ruler of the earth: yet, if any temporal advantage requires our making a suitable return to the person who bestowed the gist, what tribute can we pay to the Giver of all spiritual gifts? He requires no oblations, but what should voluntarily proceed from a good heart; such as an unisorm obedience to his holy laws and faith in his promises. We should be. zealous in the discharge of this part of our duty.

There There requires no other incitement to make us so, but a just estimate of the invaluable blessings of our creation, preservation, and redemption; a due sense of which will inspire us, to enter into his courts with joy,, and singpraises unto his holy name;

Lady *Mary,:* My dear Mentoria, you have given roe such a clear idea of my religious duty, I cannot possibly ever neglect the persormance of it. E remember, you once promised to explain, some of the parables to me:: if it be agreeable, I shalt now attend to you with pleasure. . *Mentoria* To proceed in due order, I must begin bv informing you of the nature of *parables,* and why our blessed Saviour chofe this mode pf instruction;, to enlighten the minds of his disciples, in preserence to any other. A parable is a figurative composition; and when it is notz spoken by an-inspired person, nor sound.iji'holy writ, it bears a near resemblance to apologue or fable; as the convieHon both produce arises from the moral inserences drawn from them: which, by the indirect application they make to the heart, have induced many persons of inflexible dispositions, to yield eviG 5 deuce? dence against themselves. This undoubtedly was the cause of our Saviour's delivering his: instruc-

tions in parables, as they not only engaged the attention, but surmounted the cavils and obstinacy of the Jews; which could have been effected by no other means. If he meant to convince a sinner of the heinoufness of his offence, and to lead him into the right path, by the light of the gospel; he represented in such glaring colours, the particular instance in which he erred, that the deep sense the offender had of his own guilt, obliged him instantly to forfake it, or he remained self-condemned. As there appeared no:hing perfonal in the attack, he might at sirst be enraged against the perpetrators of the very crimes he was guilty of himself: a remarkable instance of which, we sind in David, when Nathan was sent to reprove him for killing Uriah, that he might marry his wise Bathsheba.

Lady *Louisa*.

That is one of the stories I am particularly fond of: fo I hope, my dear Mentoria, you will-explain it sirst.

Lady *Mary*.

Lady Louifa, I approve your choice fo much, that, if you had not made the request, I should have done it myself.

Mentoria Mentoria. 1 will comply with your request, though it in some measure, obliges me to go in a different track from what I intended; as I propofed selecting one of our Saviour's parables, as best suited to inform you of the natnre of his ministry. Notwithstanding which, that delivered by the prophet Nathan as he was an inspired writer) deserves your praise and attention. Lady *Louisa*. Pray,, Mentoria, what is a *Prophet? Mentoria*. A Prophet was a person of exemplary conduct and holiness of lise, inspired by God with the power of soretelling events. Lord *George*. Are there any Prophets now? I think I know no body, who can fay what will happen. *Mentoria*. It is not now necessary there should be any Prophets, as God by thofe, and other means, has so clearly revealed his will, that even the most ignorant do not so much err from not knowing their duty, as because they have not resolution, to practise it. In the early ages of the world, and besore Christianity was so firmly established, prophecies and miracles were indispenfably G 6 necessary,. necessary, to remove the errors of the Pagans, and the obstinacy of the Jews. As every circumstance they foretold, agreed in unity of time and place, and came to pass exactly as they were predicted; there could be no doubt of their divine origin, as such wondersul thing could not be effected or produced by any human means.

Lady *Mary.* What are the *Pagans,* my good Mentoria*? Mentoria.* The Pagans are thofe people, whom you have perhaps heard or read of, by the name of Heathens; who worshipped idols, which consisted of men, birds, beasts, &c. I shall fay but little on this subject, as you will find it clearly explained in the Pantheon. Lord *George.* I hope, my good Mentoria, you will now begin the Parable; as I am very fond of allegorical writings.

Mentoria. I shall first recite the Parable, explain each particular branch of it, and then endeavour to find how we can apply it to ourselves. The PARABLE. ' And the Lord sent Nathan to David, and "he came and faid unto him, There were "two "two men in one city, the one rich, and "the other poor. The rich man had exceed"ing manv flocks and herds; hut the poor man "had nothing, faveone little ewe-lamb, which he had bought and nourished up; and it grew "together with him, and with his children: "it did eat of his own meat, and drank of his "own cup, and was unto him as a daughter. "And there came a traveller unto the ricb ' man, and he spared to take of his own flock, "and of his own herd, to dress for the way faring man, that was come unto him; but "took the poor man's lamb, and dressed it "for the man that was come unto him. And "David's anger was greatly kindled against "the man, and he faid to Nathan, As the "Lord liveth, the man that hath done this "thing shall surely die: and he shall restore "the lamb four-fold, because he did this thing, "and because he had no pity. And Nathan. "faid unto David, Thou art the man!" Lady *Louisa.* It is scarcely possible toimagine, as David was fo much enraged against the perfon,

who he thought had committed such an act of oppression, that he could ever have been guilty os a similar offence.. '. *Mtaloria. Mentorin.* Yet it is evident he was, and with many circumstances, which aggravate, and make his transgression appear in a more heinous light,' than that described by the Prophet. We will now consider the sirst sentence of the Parable, which strongly marks the different spheres of lise, in which David and Uriah acted. "There "were two men in one city; the one rich, "and the other poor." David was the greatest king of the East, and UriaFi comparatively poor; as he was only one of the king's officers. "The rich man had many slocks and herds." This passage alluded to the many wives that David had, as in thofe days perfons of all conditions of lise were permitted to have as many as they could maintain. The great number which David had, do not appear to have been imputed to him as a fault, but considered as a necessary appendage to his royalty. The disproportion of their outward condition is beautisully preserved throughout the whole metaphor, and is emphatically expressed in the following words: "But the poor man had "nothing, fave one little ewe-Iamb, which he "had bought and nourished up; and it grew up together with him, and'with his children i "it did eat of his own meat, and drank of "his cup, and was unto him as a daughter. " By this we sind, Uriah had but one wise; and by her being compared to a lamb, we are naturally led to suppofe, she was a woman of an amiable disposition, and exemplary conduct; as a lamb is an emblem of innocence. We are also to imagine, from the kind treatment bestowed on the lamb, that Uriah was a tender husband, and afforded Bathsheba all the comsorts and conveniences,, his situation enabled him to procure. We are now come to the passage, which describes a traveller coming unto David, in these words: "And there "came a traveller unto the rich man, and he "spared to take of his own flock, to dress for "the way-faring man that was come unto him; "but took the poor man's lamb, and dressed "it sor the man

that was come unto him." These allusions undoubtedly imply the inordinate and unruly passion, which induced David to commit such an atrocious crime. The being described as a traveller, clearly indicates it took him by surprize, and would remain his guest, but a short time. The entertainment, he is suppofed to have provided for him, is strongly expressed by the sparing his own herds, and taking. taking the poor man's Iamb; which was literally the neglecting his own wives, and setting his affections on Bath-fheba, the wife of Uriah We are now to examine the final, and most: interesting part of the story; which is the strongest instance, that can possibly be produced, of the frailty of human nature. "And: '' David's anger was greatly kindled against "the man, ami he faid to Nathan, As the "Lord livetlv the man, that has done this"thing, shall surely die;, and he shall rellore"the lamb sour-fold, because he did this thing, and because he had no pity." When David pronounced this sentence, he little suspected, it contained his own condemnationIs he had sormed the (lightest suspicion, the offence bore-arty similitude to his own condition,, he would have sound some favourable circumstance to extenuate the fault, and, consequently, to mitigate the punishment. The accusation came in such an oblique direction, therewas no possibility of his warding off the blow. The detestation he selt for the ofsender is clearly proved, by the severity of the sentence heinflicted; as four-sold restitution in kind was' all the law required. Yet, in this instance,. David thought it was not sufficient atonement,.

and: and commanded the culprit to die. The reason he alleged was this, "Because he had no "pity." Alas! where were his compassion and tender seelings flown, when he broke through every obligation, moral and divine, in destroying Uriah, that he might rival him in the affections of his wise! The truth was this; his passions had induced him to commit a crime, which, in his calmer hours, was wholly repugnant to his nature. Whilst he was engaged in the pursuit of pleasure, and surrounded with objects calculated to promote his amusement, and silence the reproaches of conscience; it is not wondersul, he had not leisure sor serious reflection. For this cause was Nathan sent unto him, as he only required a gentle admonition, to restore him to the paths of duty, from which he had strayed.

I shall now draw some inserences from the following words, in which Nathan executed his divine mission. "And Nathan faid unto David, "Thou art the man!" How surprized must David be, at so sudden and unexpected a retort! The indignation he selt, sor the oppressive conduct of the rich man, most probably employed his thoughts so entirely, it effaced the remembrance of the act of cruelty, which he himself had had committed. What remorse and compunction he must suffer, when the prophet convicted him, by the testimony of his own seelings; which were wrought upon bv no exaggerated circumstances, but only excited by the artless representation of an arbitrary and violent proceeding, committed by a person in povver, on one greatly his inserior, who was entitled to his protection, and to whom he looked sor promotion, as a reward sor his faithful services. Lady *Mary.*

I admire this Parable exceedingly, my dear Mentoria; though I cannot discover how I can apply it to myself.
Mentoria.
Nothing can be more easy, my dear Lady Mary. The moral is briesly this, and may be applied to every state and condition of lise. It stiews how blind we are to our own failings, and how quick-sighted to thofe of others. It also instructs us, when we are passing sentence, never to inslict a punishment disproportionate to the offence committed; or what, in the fame situation, we should think unreasonable to undergo ourselves.

Lady *Mary.*
I now think the moral of this Parable very applicable to Lady Louifa and myself; and sincerely sincerely hope, we shall both prosit by the excellent lesson it contains.
Mentoria. To insorce what I have al-

ready faid, I shall produce the following example, to convince your Ladyship of its farther importance and uses If your sister were guilty of any flight ofsence, and you suggested to me the necessity of her being severely punished; might I not, with great propriety, make a reply similar to that, which Nathan addressed to David? And whilst you were expatiating with vehemence on the nature of Lady Louifa's fault, I might check and silence you, entirely, by faying, " Thou "art the girl;" as most probably she is never guilty of any offence, which you have not committed at fome time or other of your lise. Let me intreat each of you to grow wise, by the example David has afforded you, nor ever subject yourselves to fo mortifying a repulse. 1 DIALOGUE VIII. MONDAY.
On the Spartan Form of Government, and System of Education, with Moral Reflections.
Lady *Louisa.*

Y dear Mentoria, did you not fome time ago promise to give us a short account oft; the *Spartan* form of Government, and plan of Education? If it is agreeable, I wish you would make them the subject of your instructions this morning.
Mentoria. My dear Lady Louifa, I will readily comply with your request; and hope you will sind the research instructive, and entertaining. Sparta, or Lacedæmon, was situated in Laconia, a part part of the Peloponnesus, now the Morea: which, with many other parts of ancient Greece, is in subjection to the Turks. Lycurgus the Legiflator of the Spartan Laws, governed the Lacedæmonians, during the minority of his Nephew. The ex cellent rules he established sor their general conduct, and the attention he paid to the instruction of their youth, have rendered his memory immortal. To prevent all disputes of precedency, he caused the whole country, and private property, to be a common stock, and divided into equal lots. It would have been difficult to have effected this, if gold and silver had not previoufly been rendered of no intrinsic value, by making the current coin of iron. This stratagem banished many

crimes from Sparta; as there was no temptation to rob another of thofe possessions which were too cumberous to be concealed. Efsectually to prevent any distinctions in the ceconomy of private families, Lycurgus established public tables, where no sood was allowed, but such as the law directed; they usually were divided into different companies, consisting of about fifteen in each class. Lord *George.* Did the Spartans like these regulations? *1%* should ftiould think it hard, if such were to take place now.
Mentoria. Thofe who had possessed great riches, and been accustomed to live luxurioufly, were so enraged at the diminution of their privileges, they rebelled, and proceeded fo far, as to pelt Lycurgus with stones: To escape their resentment, he endeavoured to seek resuge in 3 temple; he outran all his enemies, except Alcander, whofe zeal tempted him to pursue Lycurgus with speed and cruelty. As he was turning his head to form an opinion of his own fasety, this young man beat out one os his eyes with a stick. Lycurgus bore this unfortunate circumstance, with the greatest fortitude: Immediately stopping short, he shewed his face, streaming with blood, to the citizens; who were struck with the most poignant grief, and delivered Alcander to Lycurgus to be punished as he thought sit: he, instead of inslicting one adequate to his offence, took him into his house, and appointed him to the office of waiting on him as a domestic servant. This unmerited and unexpected lenity, wrought such a change in Alcander's conduct, he afterwards became one of the most distinguished citizens of Sparta; which proves the good effect of forgiving ing an injury, rather than seeking means to revenge it.
Lady *Mary.*
I am very sorry, my dear Mentoria, that Lycurgus met with such an accident, as he was so good a man.
Mentoria.
To perpetuate the memory of this unsortunate circumstance, the Lacedæmonians never after suffered a person to enter their assemblies with staff in their

hand.

Lady *Louisa*,

On what food did the Spartans chiefly live, my good Mentoria?

Mentoria.

The dish held in the highest estimation, was a kind of black broth: The old men who fat by themselves, lived entirely upon it, and left the meat to the younger part of the society.

Dionysius the tyrant, partaking of one of these repasts, complained of the insipidity of the broth. "I am not surprised (faid the cook) "the seasoning is wanting-" What seasoning? replied the Tyrant. "Hunger and thirst pro"duced by exercise of various kinds, answered "the cook, are the ingredients with which "we relish our sood."

Lord

Lord *George*. Was it not very impertinent of a servant t» speak in such a familiar manner to a king? I should think it very extraordinary, is a cook was to speak fo to me, though I am not in such an high station os lise.

Mentoria. Your Lordship mull remember, that the Spartans had levelled all distinctions in their own commonwealth; and consequently thought themselves freed from paying any great marks of obedience and respect, to those invested with power.

Lady *Mary.* Who was appointed to order what there should be for dinner?

Mentoria. There was a settled plan, which they invaribly pursued, as variety would have encouraged the luxury they meant to abolish; for which reafon their food was of the plainest kind, that they might not be tempted to eat more than was abfolutely necessary for the support of nature. Each member of the Society, contributed to the common stock, and was obliged to fend every month, sive pounds of cheese, a bushel of meal, eight gallons of wine, two pounds and an half of sigs, with a small sum of H money, money, to buy sish and meat. Whenever they offered a facrisice, they presented part of the victim to the common table; and sent a portion of all the game they killed, to the public stock, for the good of the community. Thofe who had been persorming a facrisice, or

been employed in hunting, were permitted to sup in their Own houses; no other circumstances excusing their appearance in public. Lady *Louisa*. That, I suppofe, was no hardship; as people in general, like to spend their time in company. *Mentoria.* Yet a very different plan was pursued by the Ancients; as moderation, and temperance, were their principal objects; and wisdom, the ultimate end of their wishes; the Spartans sent their children to the public tables, as to seminaries of learning, where they were to be instructed in political affairs, and acquire the art of conversing with ease and pleafantry. They were early accustomed to bear raillery, and as their fatire was very pointed, it was thought unbecoming of a Spartan, not to be able to receive a retort with compofure. They expressed their sentiments in sew words, and generally made their replies in Apophthegms, or smart smart sayings. Hence it is, a concise manner of expression is called Laconic; as Sparta was situated in Laconia, from whence the word Laconic is derived.

Lady *Mary.*

What other customs had they, my dear Mentoria?

Mentoria.

It was a general rule amongst them, whenever a perfon entered a room for the oldest member of the Society, to point to the door, and fay, "Not a word faid in this company, must go out there. " They alfo elected their associates in the following manner; each ol the company took a pellet of bread, and threw it into the pitcher, which a servant carried on his head; thofe who approved him, flung the ball in with altering the shape; whilst thofe who wished to prevent his being chofen, squeezed it flat; if there were but one of the flatted pieces in the pitcher, the candidate was rejected. Our mode of election by ballot, is nearly the fame; which consists of a number of balls, fome black, and fome white, the majority of either, determining the choice or exclusion.

H 2 Lord Lord *George.*

Lycurgus must have been a very clever man to make such excellent laws.

Mentoria.

To prevent magnificence in their houses, he ordained that their ceilings should only be wrought by the axe, and their gates and doors smoothed by the faw; presuming they would not then be so absurd to surnish their houses in an elegant taste, as it would have appeared unsuitable to the rest of the dwelling.

Lady *Louisa*.

I hope, my dear Mentoria, you have not. finished your account of the Spartans. *Mentoria.*

As far only as relates to their sorm of Government. I shall now examine the diligent and early attention they paid to the sormation of the minds of their youth, from their insancy, till they arrived at years of maturity. The Spartan children were considered as a public concern,from whom legiflators and heroes were to spring; which is the only excuse that can be offered for the cruel law in sorce amongst them that, as soon as a child was born, the father was obliged to carry it to a place called Lesche, where a council was held to examine the the insant: if it appeared healthy and wellproportioned, they allotted him one of the shares of land into which the country was divided; but on the contrary, if it was deformed or sickly, it was cast into a deep cavern, called Apothetæ. It appearing to them, neither for the good of the child, nor interest of the community, to preserve a lise that in all probability would not be serviceable to the common wealth. The Spartan nurses were held in such high estimation, they were often procured for people in foreign countries, as without swathing the children, they were straight, and well shaped. Their education was esteemed a thing of too much consequence to be trusted to the caprfee of the parents: who might, perhaps, have formed a plan, very different to that approved by the Spartan council. To prevent which, when they were about seven years os age, they were ranked in different classes, and lived together, persorming the fame exercises, and undergoing the fame discipline, and partaking of the fame recreation?. They acquired no superfluous learning; as the chief aim was to make them good subjects, to be able to endure hardships, and subdu3 their enemies. They were accustomed to go barefooted, with their heads shaved, and almost H 3 naked; naked; which inured them to the difficulties they were to undergo. After they were twelve years of age, they were not permitted to wear a double garment. They stept on beds made of reeds, gathered by the river Eurotas, and were obliged to break off the sharp points with their singers, as they were not allowed any weapons for that purpofe. To render it warm in winter, they mixed fomethistle-down with the reeds, which was thought a great indulgence.

Lady *Louisa.* I am very glad there are not such laws in England, as I should not like to live as the Spartans did.

Mmtona. A man of distinguished abilities, was chofen to super-intend the instruction of these youth; beside whom, there was to every class, a Captain, or what they called, an Irens, who was generally about twenty years of age; and whofe ofsice was to preserve order and regularity. Thofe, who were entrusted to his care, were entirely subservient to his will, and waited on him as servants. The younger ones he sent together herbs, &c. and employes thofe whowere capable of higher enterprizes, in stealing wood, and various other articles. They usually effected; effected their purpofe, when persons were afleep, or their attention deeply engaged: and if they failed in their attempt, or were caught in the fact, were severely punished. Lady *Mary.*

I think it was very wrong to teach them to steal; I dare fay, my dear Mentoria, you are of my opinion.

Mentoria.

My dear Lady Mary, you must never lofe sight of the plan of lise, sor which they were intended. As their laws were rather a political, than a moral system, this qualification might be esteemed requisite in a Spartan, whofe existence, in a great measure, was to depend on the rapine and plunder, authorized in warlike ex peditions. They possessed an uncommon share of sortitude; a remarkable instance of which, we find, in the famous story of the Spartan boy; who

being detested in the thest of a young sox, concealed it under his coat, and suffered it to tear out his bowels, rather than. make a discovery of his guilt. Lady *Louisa.*

I wonder he had such resolution, and am surprised he did not cry, when he selt it hurt him,

H 4 *Mentoria. Meritoria.*

The sense of shame was fo early instilled into their minds, it overcame all other considerations. The Spartans deserve the highest commendation, for the respect and reverence they paid to age. They shewed their elders every outward mark of obedience, always rofe from their seat when they entered, and gave place to them on all occasions; neither were they wholly conssined to the observance of forms and ceremonies; but were equally attentive to the advice and admonitions of their superiors: by which means, their conduct was proverbially wise and discreet.

Lady *Mary.* My dear Mentoria, ought we to copy the Spartans in any of their customs? *Mentoria.* It would be impossible to make them a model for your suture conduct; as the affairs of the world are now on a different footing. The Gospel was not revealed to them; consequently, their ideas of right and wrong, were only determined by the law of nature, as they had not the glorious example to imitate, which is afforded us in our blessed Saviour, and his fir stdisciples. Yet, notwithstanding you cannot follow them in the general mode of their practice. practice, pursue thofe particular branches which seem worthy of imitation; such as the reverence paid to age and wisdom; their extreme moderation and temperance in their repasts and recreations; as also the intense application with which they pursued their studies. In every age and country, the exertion of these qualities, will, produce the fame effect; and lender a Briton as famous now, as a Spartan was, several, hundred years ago. Lord *George.*

I wish, my good Mentoria, you would not quite clofe your account of the Spartans. *Mentoria.*

As I have not omitted any material circumstance; in the continuation of the

subject, I shall/ be reduced to the necessity of enlarging on what 1 have already enumerated. I have insormed you, how highly the Spartan nurses were esteemed; it now only remains for me to point out what gained them such reputation. They took insinite pains to render the insants healthy and robust; yet their excellence chiefly consisted in the attention they paid to the sormation of their dispofition and manners.

H 5 Lady

Lady *Louisa.* What particular methods did they make ufe of, my dear Mentoria?

Mentoria. They never indulged the children in fretsul and petulant inclinations, and paid no regard to their tears and idle fancies; which entirely discourages the bad habit of caprice and discontent.

Lady *Mary.* I am surprised all nurses do not act the fame I will advise my little sister's nurse to treat her in this manner.

Mentoria. Without vanity, Lady Mary, I may venture to affirm, I understand the Sparian manners,better than any nurse: fo, that with more propriety, I shall be able to adopt this plan, in the regulation of your conduct. I should think, I was acting a very weak, as well as a very wicked part, if I indulged all your desires; and should not discharge my duty, without I corrected your errors, and pointed out the means to amend them. Lady *Louisa.*

What were they remarkable for besides? *Mentoria.*

To prevent the children being dainty, they

fed sed them on very plain food; and accuflomed them to eat all kinds of provision, that they might not have a particular diflike to any. Lady *Mary.* I should think it very hard to be obliged to eat what I did not like. *Mentoria.* When a perfon has a natural and strong aversion to anv particular thing, it would be cruel to oblige them to partake of it; in such a case I would not exert my authority: but if it eared to be the effect of prejudice or caprice, I would use the strongest effort to surmount the difficulty. I could produce many instances of children, fancying they did not like different parts of their food; which, when they had been compelled, or prevailed on to taste, were extremely agreeable to them. This, like most bad habits, makes a rapid progress, if it be not checked in its insancy; which proves how jndicious it was of the Spartans, to guard against such a growing evil. Lady *Louisa.* 1 will never be dainty for the suture, and never leave any orts on my plate. *Mentoria.* The branch I am now going to consider, will, I hope, prove an usesul lesfon to you both; as H 6 it it points at your greatest weakness; namely,. *Fear.* The Spartans were so undaunted in their nature, they trained up their children,. without any sense of unnecceflary apprehensions j to effect which, they accustomed them to be alone, and in the dark, to prevent their being timorous and cowardly. Lady *Lout/ar.*

I wish I could get the better of all my sears, and be as easy in the dark as I am in the light. *Mentoria.* ..

I can ascribe Fear but to two causes, which. are these; the consciousness of deserving punishment, or the prejudicesimbibed in infancy. I impute your sears to the latter, which may he overcome by the exertion of your own reason, and confidence in the assertions of your best friends. The errors which have been irtililled into your minds, are so palpable, they are easily consuted; as there requires little to be faid, to convince you, ghosts, fairies, and hobgoblins, are creatures of the imagination, 'which have no existence but in weak and unenlightened minds!

Lady *Mary.*

Yet, my dear Mentoria, who can deny darkness being difagreeable?

Mentoria:. Mentoria.

It does not appear the least sormidable to me.

I have no sears or apprehensions then, more than at noon-day, as I consign my self with trust confidence into the hands of my Creator, to»

whom darkness and light are both alike. Guilt is the only darkness which can disturb our peace; and Innocence, the only light which can dispel our Fears! To ensorce what I have already said, I will repeat a few lines I wrote on this subject.

On FEAR.

Avaunt, vain FeJr, thou phantom of the mind.

Stranger to inward peace, to reason blind!

Thou Ignis Fatuus, which misleads the sense;.

Against thy inroads, where is the desence?

The shield of Faith, can best defy thy sway;

Ward off thy blows, and tby sharp stings

allay.

Thou coward, passion, of ignoble birth, Whofe utmost limits are confin'd to earth;

In heaven, I trust, thy lawless pow'r will cease,

Th' abode of Angels, Harmony, and Peace.

Lady *Louisa.*

I know a phantom is an imaginary evil, 'which haunts the fenses, such as ghosts, fairies,.

ries, &c. but do not comprehend the meaning of the words, *Ignes Fatuu.* *Mentoria.* They are derived from the Latin, and mean false sire. Hence it is, the meteor, commonlycalled, *Will with a wisp,* takes that name. Lady *Mary.* For what reafon, my dear Mentoria? *Mentoria.* Because, notwithstanding it is a vapour or exhalation of the earth, it has a luminous appearance; and often leads travellers out of the right path, by their mistaking it for the light in a cottage, or fome other dwelling. Lady *Mary.* But what resemblance can you possibly sind between this phænomenon and Fear? *Mentoria.* I shall foon convince you of the likeness, by pointing out, that they are equally delusive, and produce nearly the'fame consequences. The meteor carries thofe, who are unfortunate enough to be misted by its influence, far from the place of their destination; whilst Fear leads thofe, who are under its dominion, into the labyrinth of folly and superstition.

Lady *Louisa.* But, my dear Mentoria, where is the shield of of faith, which desends us from Fear? I wish I possessed it.

Mentoria. Virtues are often figuratively

compared to different parts of armour, to imply, that they fortify us against the asfaults we meet with in our warsare upon earth. Faith is, sor this reason, stiled the shield; as faith or considence in God, is the only desence which can screen us from the attacks of our enemies, or the dread of an impending evil. Thus St. Paul advised his disciples to gird themselves with Truth, and to have their seet shod with the Gofpel; but above all, to take the shield of Faith, which he expressly told them would be able to quench the fiery darts of the wicked. Righteousness be compared to a breast-plate, Salvation to a helmet. The word of God, he also emphatically called, the sword of the Spirit, and the whole accoutrements, the Armour of God, in which every Christian ought to be clothed. Lady *Mary.*

Pray, Mentoria, what is *Superftition?* *Mentoria.*

Superstition causes Fear; and proceeds either from credulity, or the prejudices of education. It is of various kinds; the errors of the Roman Church are a principal branch; as their tenets, nets, are sounded on a system of pretended miracles, and supernatural events. There i. another species of a less fatal tendency; namely, the belies of divination, faith ia omens, or any mystical process, such as sortune-tellers, conjurers, &c. Thofe whofe minds are weak, enough to pay attention to such, fallacious, guides, and have strong confidence in theis predictions, naturally grow timid, and degenerate from their original purity. Lady *Louisa*

What will cure Superstition, and prevent its having a strong influence on our minds? *Mentoria..*

Good sense and Superstition are irreconcileable enemies; when they enter into single combat, the farmer generally comes off victorious.

Hence, Superstition! hide thy daring head,.

By weak distrust, and human folly bred! Subdu'd by fense, the victor of thy fate, In chains thou, shalt appear to grace her state!

Lady *Mary..* Are not ignorant people, my dear Mentoria,. generally the most superstitious?

Mentoria. Mentoria. Undoubtedly; because Superstition is the natural consequence of ignorance. As the fun dispels darkness, so does knowledge clear the understanding from the mists of error and delusion. Let me entreat you to avoid the fetters of ignorance; as the chains which confine the mind, is the worst flavery a human creature can experience. Yet, unlike most other bonds, they may be broken by the strong efforts of our reason.

Oh Ignorance! thou chaos of the mind!

TV eclipse of reason, to improvement blind.

Thou, like the owl, dost shun the glorious light,

Enwrapp'd in darkness, and the shades of night.

All pow'rsul science does dispel thy gloom;

Makes thee expire, and rest within the tomb.

Erects a trophy o'er thy mould'ring dust
Of highest polish, cleans'd siom soulest rufH

Lady *Louisa.* My dear Mentoria, do you think I shall soon be able to make verses on any subject? I wish you would teach me.

Mentoria. I shall be content, my dear Lady Louifa, if you are able to express your sentiments with ease and elegance in *Prose.* This can only be acquired acquired by practice. We all lisp before we can speak, and walk before we can dance; for which reafon be not discouraged, though your productions abound with errors. Do not repeat thofe you have already committed, and thev will every day decrease. An opportunity now ofsers for you to exert your skill; as affection will suggest to you, the necessity of insorming Lady L. of the pleasing event which happened yesterday. First, form the substance of your letter, and then clothe it in as agreeable a dress as possible. I would recommend to your Ladyship, to pay the fame attention to the adorning your sentiments, as you would bestow on the decoration of your perfon. You must be guided in the latter by fashion and the caprice of the times: in the former, by the immutable and un-

changeable rules of orthography and good sense.

Lady *Louisa.*

But what shall I fay, my dear Mentoria?

Mentoria.

You would not ask me that question, if she came to pay you a visit: imagine yourself engaged in converfation with her, and you will not then be at a lofs. Epistolary correspondence is nothing more than an exchange of sentiments, which ought to be delivered with as much ease and and freedom as is usually authorized in common discourse, with only this distinction, thatwe should pay rather more attention to our manner of expression; and be particularly caresul to avoid tautology, or the repetition of words; because our errors appear more palpable, when they are recorded, and may yield evidence against us. Divest yourself of unnecessary sears, and cheer yourself with the pleasing reflection, that your best endeavours (even if the persormance is impersect) will be accepted, and entitle you to applause.

DIALOGUE IX. TUESDAY.

On the Sciences; with a general Exhortation to acquire Knowledge.

Mentoria. T ADY Mary, you once requested me t« """ insorm you of the nature of I he *Sciences,* which I then declined; if your curiofity is not abated by delay, we will now examine them with the attention they deserve. Lady *Mary.* Mv desire to be acquainted with their difserent qualities, is now as strong as when I made the request. Are there not seven Sciences, my dear Mentoria?

Mentoria. Yes, my dear. I shall consider them in regular order; and consequently begin with *Grammar, Grammar,* on which the principles of every language depend.

Lady *Louisa.*

My dear Mentoria, you need not fay much about Grammar, as we understand it very well. I could answer you any questions you chuse to ask me.

Mentoria.

To put it to the proof, what is a *Noun?*

Lady *Louisa-.* Are not the words man, house, joy, sorrow, all nouns?

Mentoria. You are persectly right, my dear Lady Louifa, but let me hear your reasons sor suppofing them so.

Lady *Louisa.* Because, by prefixing an *article* they make sense.

Mentoria. They are also of two kinds, the *nounsubslantive,* and the noun *adjeclive.* Let me hear you explain them, my dear Lady Mary. Lady *Mary.* A noun substantive is the name of a thing without any reserence to its peculiar qualities: Example.—*The man;* but a noun adjective denotes the properties of the object it expresses, as os in the following instances: a *good* man, a *large* house, in which it plainly appears the words *good* and *large* are the adjectives.

Mentoria. My dear Lady Mary, it gives me infinite pleasure to find you such a good grammarian. In order more sully to explain the rudiments of this usesul science, I shall insorm you, they principally consist of the different *moods* and *tenses,* which may be divided into the sollowing classes: the *pa/l, (hepresent,* and the *future,* denoting our powers of action. Lady *Louisa.* I wish you would explain them, my dear Mentoria. *Mentoria.* I shall begin by insorming you the word *tense* signifies the time in which we speak or act; and the *mood* implies the manner. The *indicative* mood affirms, or is positive. Example: "I am, thou art, he is, &c." Lady *Mary.* I hope you will produce somemore instances.

Mentoria. There are many of the moods and tenses so plain, you cannot mistake their meaning. I will endeavour to enumerate thofe which I think think require fome explanation: The *potential* mood denotes power. Example: "as I may, can, or could walk." The *imperative* mood implies authority, or command: for instance, "Have thou, let him have, let us be, &c." The *optative* mood clearly indicates a wish to obtain, which is as follows: "That I may have, that thou may est have, that he may have." The *infinitive,* which is the last of the moods, presuppofes, and requires a verb, or part of a phrase to precede it, in order to make the sense complete. Example: " I desire to read;" the infinitive " to read," would not be sense without the word desire. I shall fay no more on this subject, as you acquire this usesul knowledge in the common course of your lesfons, and already know the use of the different parts of speech, which consist of the *noun, article, pronoun, adjetlive, verb, participle, adverb, preposition, conjunilion,* and *interjeclion.* I shall now, therefore, proceed to explain the other sciences.

Lady *Mary.*

Which is the next you mean to discourse upon?

Mentor ia. Logic, or the art of reasoning, is an abstruse study, but of insinite use to divines and lawyers; lawyers; as it enables them to explain mysterious subjects, and reconcile seeming absurdities.

Lord *George-.* That must be a difficult task, how can they possibly do it?

Mentoria. By tracing consequences to the cause which produces them, however remote and imperceptible to common observers; by which means they refute errors, and convince the unbelieving. Lord *George.*

How do they effect such wondersul things?

Merit or ia. By demonstration, or positive proof: for instance, you would laugh if a Logician told you "snow was black," which he would prove, by insorming you that the water was black; and that snow is but water congealed. You would then agree in the belies of what he affirmed, and be encouraged to make researches of the fame nature; this is what is called a *paradox.* There is another sigure of speech called a *syllogism,* which consists of three parts, the major, the minor, and the consequence. Example: First, if there is a king, he ought to I be *be* feared; secondly, there is a king; which, thirdly, implies he must be searedLady *Mary.* Is this science of great use, my dear Mentoria? Arithmetic. This science comprehends the use and properties of figures, and consequently is part of the Mathematics. The sour first rules, namely, *addition, Jubtraclion, multiplication,* and *division,* are very necesfary parts of your education. If you are defective in these points, you would not be qualified to regulate your affairs, when you come to

years of maturity. *Mentor ia.* Yes, my dear, particularly in all theological or divine writings, learned arguments, and deep researches.

Lady *Louisa.* What is the next science, my dear Menloria?

Mentoria. Rhetoric or the art of eloquence and persuasion.

Lord *George.* Are Logic and Rhetoric, alike in any respects?

Mentoria. Not in the least. Logic investigates the truth by axioms, or self-evident principles; but Rhetoric by a fair assemblage 'of words, and well tuned periods, often causes us to viewcircumstances through a false medium, and consequently induces us to applaud what we ought to condemn. The powers of eloquence and flowers of rhetoric are irresistible; and when they proceed from a good heart, and «tr.e exerted in a good cause, arc highly deserving ing of our praise and admiration. This quality is indispenfably necesfary, for all public speakers, but more particularly fo to lawyers, as the success of the cause they undertake to plead, frequently depends on nice distinctions,

intricate points of law, and the narration of facts, which require the graces of speech, and delicate strokes of elocution.

Lady *Louisa.*

How does Rhetoric make people eloquent?

Mentoria.

By enabling them to express their sentiments according to the rules of art; and to adorn them with the sigures of speech called

tropes, metaphors, allegories, hyperboles, &x.

that are nothing more than mental ornaments, on which the internal beauty depends,

as much as the external does on dress and exterior decorations. As they neither of them produce an happy effect, if they are not properly dispofed, the one should be blended with truth,

the other with simplicity and nature. I mall now explain the extensive and usesul science of *Arithmetic.*

Lady *Mary.* We learn that of our writing-master, and therefore know what it

means. *Mentoria.* What he teaches you, is a part of Simple 1 2 V Arithmetic.

Lady *Louisa.* You fay we are taught *Simple Arithmetic,* what other sort is there my good Mentoria? *Mentoria.* The more abstruse part of the science is called *Algebra,* in which letters are used instead of sigures, to solve the problems, and ascertain their product, which is of great importance to Mathematicians. Lady *Mary.* What are the other sciences, my dear Mentoria?

Mentoria. The next that will engage our attention is *Geometry,* which is also a principal branch of the Mathematics, and includes whatever is capable of mensuration. Geometrical problems are very entertaining, they teach rules of proportion, and the use of various figures, such such as circles, ovals, angles, triangles, quadrangles or squares, octagons, heptagons, hexagons, pentagons, parallel lines, cubes, &c.. Lady *Louisa.*

What are the meaning of these words, and from whence are they derived? *Mentoria.*

From the Latin and Greek. The word Circle signifies round, and is derived from *circus,* a ring; Oval, from *ovum,* an egg, as it bears that form; Angle, from *angulus,* a corner, as i.t implies the meeting of two lines; Triangle, from *tres,* three, and *angulus,* corner, as it has three sides; and consequently Quadrangle from *quatuor* and *angulus,* as it has sour sides. These are all derived from the Latin.

Lady *Maryi .. ..*sercnt de iraei

The others take their different delations' from the Greek.

Mentoria. j

Yes, my dear Lady Mar)', the word *OBagon* means eight sides; I believe the *Heptagon* has the fame etymology, which has seven sides; *Hexagon* which has six; and *Pentagon* which has five. *Parallel* is taken from the Greek, and means even with each other, yet cannot meet: hence it is, parallel lines imply being at an equal distance. The word *Cube* or Square,

I 3 is From *firra,, fecen,* and *ywitt, a corner.* is also derived from the Greek, and signifies a die, which is the singular of dice, as it is the fame length, width, and depth, and on every side sorms an exact square. I have drawn a sketch of these difserent figures, which, X hope, will be of suture service to you, exemplified in plate II.

Lady *Louisa.* I should like to learn *Geometry,* it seems very entertaining.

Mentoria. It is not a part os semale education, neither can you sorm a proper judgment from the sketch I have given, any more than you would be enabled to understand a language by only seeing the alphabet. I shall now take a cursory or flight view of *Astronomy,* which teaches the situation or motion of the heavenly bodies. This science, from the clofe connection it has with Geography, may properly be called its counter, part.

Lady *Mary.* What are the *Heavenly Bodies,* my dear Mentoria?

Mentoria. The Sun, Planets, Constellations, &c. The orb of light called the *Sun,* is fixed in the midst of the universe, and is supposed to persorm a a revolution a revolution on its own axis from west Jo east once in twenty sive clays; it always shines with the fame lustre, and gives light and heat to the whole planetary system. Its diameter is about eight hu-ndred thoufand miles.

Lady *Louisa.* What are *Planets,* my dear Madam? *Mentoria.* They move round the Sun, in a constant and regular course. *Mercury,* which is the least of the primary planets, is next to the Sun,, at the distance of about thirty two millions of miles, and is computed to be two thoufand four hundred and sixty miles in diameter, and persorms its revolution round ther Sun, in eighty-eight days. The planet *Venus, fs* next to Mercury, and is suppofed to be about the size of the Earth, which is computed to be seven thousand nine hundred and sixtv miles in diameter, and she persorms her course in the space of two hundred twenty four days and an half, at the distance of sifty nine millions of miles from the sun. These are stiled' the inserior planets, because their process is between the earth and ft.

Lady *Mary.*. I remember, my dear. Mentoria, in your account of Geography,, you insormed us the *Earth,* was a plan-

et, and moved round the sun, i-fc *'Mentaria. Mentoria.*

You are perfectly right, my dear Lady. Mary. TheEarth is distant frem the Sun about eighty ne millions of miles, is rather more than seven thoufand nine hundred and sixty miles irtrfiameter, and persorms its revolutions round the sun in 365 days, which constitutes our solar year. The *Moon* is considered as a secondary planet, and is ever attendant on the Earths at the distance ef two hundred and forty thoufand miles. She is computed to be fifty times less than the Earth, and persorms, her course round it in-the space of a month. Lady *Louisa.*

We can perceive her process by the light she affords us at some times, which at others is hidden from us. *Mtntoria.*

We must now consider the superior planets, which are so named, because they are either above, or encompass that of the Earth. The first is *Mars.:* its diameter is about sour thousand four hundred miles, and its distance from the sun about one hundred and twenty three millions. Its revoluAin round the sun, is persormed in two years wanting forty three days. Next to Mars is *Jupiter.* which is the largest of all the planets. Its diameter. is rather above eighty eighty one thoufand miles, and is distant from the sun about four hundred millions. It performs its course round the sun in twelve years, excepting about sifty days, and is suppofed to revolve on its own axis in the short space of ten hours. This planet is constantly attended by four moons, usually called *satellites,* which appear in a direst line with this great orb. Next, and lastly, we sind the planet *Saturn*: its diameter is computed to be about sixty eight thoufand mileSj and its distance from the sun seven hundred and seventy seven millions of miles, and persorms its revolution round the sun in the space of twenty nine years and an half. It is attended by sive moons, and a ring of great magnitude, which has a luminous appearance. The distances-and diameters of theplanets, which I have just recited, have beeir demonstrated by fome of the best as-

tronomers;. but if the observations on the transit of Verm may be depended on, it requires one-sixth part of each number to be added to the number itself, in order to ascertain the real dimensions of all the planets, except the earth.. These divine luminaries, are in themselves dark or opaque bodies, and transmit to us th light of the sun by reflection.

I &., Lordi

Lord *George.*

I am impatient to hear what *Constellations* are; I suppofe they are stars, my dear Mentoria?

Mentoria.

They are *Jixed Jlars,* because they always preserve the fame distances, and are situated in that part of the Heavens called the *Zodiac,* which is the space where the sun and planets persorm their respective revolutions. The principal Constellations are the *Signs* of the zodiac, which are as sollows: *aries* the ram, *ianrui* the bull, *gemini* the twins, *cancer* the crab, *leo* the lion, *virgo* the virgin, *libra* the scales, *J'corpio* the scorpion, *Jagittarius* the archer, *capricornus* the goat, *aquarius* the water-bearer, and *pijces* the fishes. There are, besides these, fifty-seven Constellations, twenty nine situated on the north, and twenty eight on the south side of the zodiac. The fixed stars do not shine by reflection, but by native light, which is designed to cheer the utmost bounds of the creation.

Lady *Louisa.*

Have not I heard of *Comets,* my good Mentoria, are they not something very wondersul in the Heavens?

Mentoria. Mentoria.

They are *blazing stars,* which but rarely appear, because their revolutions round the sun are exceedingly eccentric, and persormed at such an immense distance from it, that they take an infinitude of time to complete their course, notwithstanding, their progress is very rapid. Lady *Mary.*

My dear Mentoria, you, have not *yet* mentioned the great number of stars which spangle the Heavens, how many do you think there may be.?

Mentoria.

They are ranked in different classes according to their respective magnitude;

and in Plamstead's catalogue they are computed to be in number about three thoufand and one,. notwithstanding which, there is great reason to think there are an infinitude, which elude the keenest search, and exceed the bounds of human discovery or comprehension. Lady *Louisa.*

I wonder how big.the Sun is? *Mentoria..*

It is computed.to be about eight hundred thoufand miles in diameter, my dear Lady Louifa 1-6' Lady Lady *Mary.* What is *Diameter,* my dear Mentoria? *Mentoria.*

It implies to go through the middle or centre of any tiling, in a direct line,-either from top to bottom, or from side to side.

Lady *Louisa.*

It is the fame as *Circumference,* I suppose.

Mentoria. Not in the least, as Circumserence means to go entirely round an object, and Diameter across it, which makes a very essential difference in the dimensions. It may be usesul to insorm you, that *Magnitude* means size or' bigness; *Plenitude* suhiefs; and *Altitude* the' height of any thipg. Lady *Mary.*

How much less is the earth than the sun?

Mentoria. You may easily calculate, when you recoI«. lect the earth is about seven thoufand nine hundred and sixty miles in diameter, and the sun eight hundred thoufand miles. You must alfo remember, the planet we inhabit, is computed to be eighty one millions of miles distant from the sun.

Lord *George.* I am astonished, at so very great a distance that that we can perceive its light, or seel the power of its rays!

Mentoria.

Notwithstanding we are so far from it, the inhabitants of that part of the earth which is. situated under the meridian of the sun, can scarcely endure the heat, which would be insupportable if they were placed but a sew degrees nearer to it. In this, as in every other part of the creation, the wisdom of God is manisested. "The heavens declare his glory, «' and the firmament fheweth his handy

work!' Lady *Louisa.* limagine *AJlronomy* is a very usesul science, to whom is it particularly so? *Mentoria.*

To mariners, philofophers, and' mathema-. ticians. It is also necessary sor persons of education, to pay some attention to this study, as it enlarges the ideas, and enables them to form a just conception of the Deity. The contemplation of the heavens, inspires a rational mind with wonder and admiration, which naturally produce gratitude a-nd adoration, the only acceptable offerings to the beneficent author of these inestimable blessings I Lady *Mary.*

Is not *Mujic* the next and the last science, you intend to explain my dear Mentoria?

Mentoria. Mentoria. Yes, my dear Lady Mary, yet I sear it will: not be in my power to give you a clear idea, of Music, as a person ought to be an adept, or deeply skilled in the art to attempt an explana-rtion of this pleasing science. which comprehends the power of harmony, and may be divided into two parts, *vocal* and *instrumental.* The excellence of the-composition,, depends on the proper arrangements of different notes,, some of which, from their respective qualities,, are called *flats,* and *oihersJJiarps,* which produce variation of sound, and constitute native,, as well as artificial Music. The-common scale of music, which consists of various characters to express the different notes, is called the *Gamut.* No person can excel in. this art, without a good ear; as the observation of time, and distinction of sound, arenecesfary sor every persormer, without which, they would produce discord instead of harmonys. One of the chies principles of Music, depend on what is called Concord (which signifies agreement) if this were, not attended to, it would be impossible to play in concert,, every person having the same notes, notwithstanding different parts are allotted to each;; cooseqjiently the flightest omission or encroachment. croachment would cause consusion, and spoil the whole effect.

Lady *Mary.*

I love Music very jnuch, yet sear L shall: never excel.

Mentoria.

My dear Lady Mary, the force of genius is very powersul, and generally produces in every art, a greater degree of persection, than can be acquired by any other means. Thofe who are desective in this point, must have recourse to the assistance of art, which, by the aid of industry and perseverance, proves a good substitute for genius. A taste for Music, like a taste for most other things, in many perfons is not natural, but acquired. We are guided in most of our pursuits, by the advice or example of our companions;. if they are studious, musical, or ingenious, it excites emulation in us, to engage in the fame course, and pursue the fame plan. It is reported of the chamelion, that he takes the colour of the object which is nearest to him, and consequently appears of various hues. We partake more of his nature, than at sirst sight we are apt to imagine, and are strongly tinctured with either the good or bad qualities of those with whom we asfociate.

Lady Lady *Louisa.*

I wish, my dear Mentoria, I understood alb the sciences, how wise and clever I should be! *Mentoria.*

My dear Lady Mary, knowledge like power, beyond a certain degree, subjects thofe who possess it, to many temptations and inconveniences. There requires great fortitude to ba proof against the shouts of applause bellowed on merit, and the respect and obedience which is paid to grandeur. There are very few who would not turn giddy,, if they wera transported to the summit of a high mountain, and could scarcely discern the valley beneath. In like manner thofe, who by birth or abilities, are exalted above the common class, are too apt to make no other use of their preeminence, than to look down with disdain on their inseriors. Wisdom and power can never be deemed blessings, unless, like the sun, the forr mer enlightens that part of the creation which 16 in ignorance or darkness, and the latter, cheers and enlivens those who are chilled by the blasts of poverty and oppression:!. Lady *Mary..*

Should we not wish to be praised, my

dear Mentoria, when w.e excel in any thing?

Mentoria. Mentoria.

The love of praise is not only pardonable, but commendable, as far as it proves an encitement to act so as to deserve it. It is only blameable when we make it the motive of our actions, and receive more pleasure from the applause bellowed on a good action, than we did from the silent testimony of the heart when we persormed it: seek not the approbation of men, but of God, and be assured your Father, who seeth in secret, will reward you openly.

Lady *Louisa.*

I think, if I understood all the things you *do,* my good Mentoria, I should like to (hew my knowledge, and talk of them in company. I am surprised that you do not. *Mentoria.*

If I did, it would make me ridiculous; knowledge ought not wholiy to be concealed, yet, like beauty, it appears most amiable, 'when it is seen through the veil of diffidence and modesty. If you excelled in any art or science, you should not make it the subject of your discourse, or in common converfation express your sentiments in the terms of art belonging to it; ris it would make you appear pedantic dantic and ostentatious. I once was acquainted with a gentleman, who was a great mathematician, whenever I was in company with him, he always used the fame expressions,, which differed very little from geometrical problems. When he was asked if he chofe cream in his tea, this was his constant answer: "Yes, "Ma'am, because the globular particles of the "cream, render the acute angles os the tea more obtuse." This reply might be tolerably well received for the first time, but from the repetition, and being often ill-timed, disgusted, A mere prosessional character is always difagreeable. If I were perpetually talking to you of the declension of nouns, or the idioms of the French language, would you not think me a very tiresome companion? how grave you would look, if I insisted besore you. eat a cake of your insorming me whether it was of an octagon or pentagon sorm. Thereare many times I would

entirely divest myself of the instructor, to partake of your recreations, and be considered in no other light than your friend!

Lord *George.* What did the gentleman mean by the *globular* particles of the cream, rendering the *acute angles* of the tea more obtuse?

Mcntaria.. Mentoria.

It is a generally received opinion, that all soft liquors, such as oil, cream, &c. are composed of round, or globular particles, which cause that smoothness in their taste; whilst, on the contrary, acids, such as vinegar, &c. consist o£ acute or sharp particles, which make them irritate the palate: hence he suppofed the richness of the cream would render the roughness f the tea more obtuse, which means blunt. Lady *Mary.*

I hope, my good Madam, you are not going to take leave of us sor this morning! *Mentoria.*

It gives me infinite pleasure, my dear Lady Mary, to find you so attentive to my instructions: and as Lady Louifa and Lord George areequally so, I must bestow the fame commendations-on them. To excite in your minds a desire to attain all possible persection in knowledge and virtue, I shall subjoin an exhortation to this laudable purpofe, which I sent some time ago to an amiable youth at Eton, entreating him to profecute his studies with assiduity and attention.

Goon, dearyouth, deep learning's path pursue, And keep her golden, treasures still in view:

Search.

Search with attention, sor the shining ore

Its latent qualities with care explore.

Learn all their disferent properties and use,

And gain the depth of subjects most abstruse.

Fair science is the clue by which we find

Th' intricate lab'rinth of the human mind.

Peruse great nature's b»ok, and her wise laws,

And in each page, trace the creative cause!

This will expand and animate thy hopes, When systems fail, or high exalted tropes.'

With caution six, and choofe the better part.

Ever maintain integrity of heart:.'

Let sympathetic seelings urge thee strong,

To acts of kindness, never in the wrong.

Be this the structure of thy future plan-,.

And dedicate to God, the temple— ManT

Lady *Louisa.* But these lines, my dear Mentoria, can onlyr be a lesson to Lord George, as you wrote them to a young gentleman!

Mentoria. They are (if I may be allowed the expression) *epicene* instructions, and in their tendency of general use to both sexes. I earnestly eatreat you to regulate your conduct by the plan therein propofed. Think learning to be the best riehes can you acquire, and the works of nature the the best lesson you can study. Feel sor the distresses of others, and be ever inclined to redress their grievances. Be guided in all your actions by the dictates of conscience, and the precepts of your holy religion. Dedicate your whole lise to the service of God, which will entitle you to receive the reward promised to his faithsul servants, namely, eternal lise and happiness! r DIALOGUE X

W E D N ESDI Y.

On the relative Duties of Life, with a general Exhortation to Virtue.

Lady *Mary.* MY dear Mentoria, I hope your discourse this morning will be on an entertaining 'subject.

Mentoria. I wish it to engage your attention, as from its great importance it will require your serious consideration. Some days ago, I pointed out to you your *religious* duties, or thofe you owe to your Creator. It now remains sor me to enumerate *S* enumerate the *moral* and *relative* Duties, all perfons are bound to discharge to their sellowcreatures.

Lady *Louisa.*

Why are they called *relative Duties?*

. *Mentoria.*

Because they comprehend the different classes and degrees of duty, respect, or love, which are due to thofe, who are connected with us, either by blood, friendship, or dependence; such as parents, brothers, sisters, masters, servants, friends, &c. This Duty is fo diffusive, it may be traced in regular gradation, from the monarch who sits on the throne, to the most inconsiderable of his subjects. I shall therefore consine myself to the consideration os thofe particular branches, which seem best suited to your age, and station in lise. Lady *Mary.*

I hope, my dear Mentoria, you will explain.each of these branches separately. *Mentoria.*

With great pleasure, my dear Lady Mary. The Duty we owe to our *parents,* bears a near resemblance to that which is due to our Creator; as it consists of gratitude, obedience, and love. The blessings of our creation, preservation, lion, and redemption, produce religious faith,

and impel the mind to adore and worship the

Cause from whence they proceed. In like manner, as we derive out existence from our earthly parents, and owe our fasety, and improvement to their tenderness and love, tVhich in the helpless state of insancy, we could not acquire by any oiher means) we are bound to render them the tribute of gratitude, by paying implicit obedience to their commands.

Lady *Louisa.*

I think we should be very ungratesul, if we did not regard our parents, who express such anxiety for otfr welfare, and take such infinite pains to make us accomplished.

Mcntoria.

Our obligations are so numerous, it is impossible to six their bounds; neither can I propofe any better method, as a rule for your actions, than to be unisormly obedient in your conduct. Observe and practise what is particularly pleasing to your parents? avoid thofe things which are not agreeable to them; and,

upon every 'occasion, testify your love and duty.

Lord *George.*

What is the difference between *love* and *duty,* my dear Mentoria?

K' *Mentoria. Mentoria.* They are separate qualities, yet are generally united in a moral or religious sense; which implies, that acts of obedience or duty ought to proceed from love; as sear, or the hope of reward, (if they were the motive) would make the persormance rather a facrisice than an offering.

Lady *Mary.* What distinction is there between an *offering* and *sacrifice? MentoriaAn* Ofsering is a voluntary gift bestowed on merit, or presented as a token of our gratitude and esteem: but a Sacrisice implies compulsion and reluctance; as the ceremonies to which they allude were very different in their tendency. An Ofsering usually consisted of garlands, incense, &c. a Sacrissice, of a victim cither burnt or slain, which, in the Jewish f and Pagan laws, was required as an expiation for any capital offence, or as an acknowledgment for any great advantage received. Lady *Louisa.* But how can we make amends for their kindness, when we have nothing to bestow on our parents?

Mentoria. Mentoria. In the regular course of things, it frequently happens, that parents are brought to an infirm and helpless state, and reduced to a second state of insancy: in such cases, a child is enabled to discharge the debt, by the fame means it received it. But as these instances are not very common, there is another opponunity, which proceeds from a less calamitous cause, though it demands our tenderness, and excites our compassion. I mean the gradual decline of lise, which requiras little attentions, that.'ire often more acceptable than important services; as, like a gentle shower, they revive the withered plant, which requires the prop 'of filial affection to support it. Lord *George.* Should we do every thing our parents command? If they required us to persorm what was unreasonable, or blameable, ought we to comply with their request? *Mentoria.* There is little danger of a parent leading a child into error by design: whenever they mistake the means of their advantage or happiness, the desect is in their judgment. As, in general, parents are too apt to err on the side K2 of of ten-

derness, children should in every instance consorm, and be subservient to their will. Our blessed Saviour, notwithstanding the divinity of his nature, (which, in some degree, made him independent of his parents) in various instances manisested his filial affection; and we are expressly told, he was subject to them..Let me entreat you to make his obedience, as well as every other virtue he possessed, the model sor your conduct. Imitate his example, and be guided by his precepts; write his instructions on the tablet of thy heart, which will be legible in all thy actions, and make thee au usesul member of society.

Lady *Louisa.*

Pray, Mentoria, what is our Duty to our *brothers zvAJiJlers?* I suppofe w.e are.to love, and be kind to them.

Mentoria.

You are bound to respect thofe who are older than yourself; and to instruct and protect those who are younger. You should treat' them on all occasions with tenderness and love; nor ever seek an opportunity to dipute with, or tease them. Be also particularly cautious to set a good example, to excite emulation in rthofe who are your 'elders, and to afford a pattern pattern worthy of imitation to thofe who are younger.

Lady *Mary.*

I ought, I suppofe, to love to hear them praised. t *Mentoria.*

You should alfo seek every opportunity to commend them, and not enumerate every trifling ofsence: neither are ypu to think, any praise bestowed on them derogates from your merit. This folly is painted in glowing colours, in the parable of the *prodigal son.* The father, when the prodigal returned, met him with every token of joy, and caused the fatted calf to he killed. The elder brother, who was in the sield, when he heard the found of music, enquired what event had happened, to cause such acclammations of joy; the history insorms us, he was displeased, when he found it was to celebrate his brother's arrival, and resolved not to go into the house. His father expostulated with him on the occasion, and intreated him to partake of the sestivity his brother's return had occasioned; which had no effect on his obdurate heart. On the contrary, he upbraided his father for never bestowing on him even a kid, to make merry with his friends: K 3 though though when his fon returned, who had wasted; his substance with riotous living, he gave him even the fatted calf. He then proceeded to exaggerate his brother's transgressions, and to enumerate the advantages his father had delived from his own faithsul services; which, however true, came but with an ill grace from his own testimony, and greatly took from the merit of the persormance. The tender parent, stung with the reproaches of his child, endeavoured to obviate the charge of injustice and partiality, in the following words: " Son, thou "art ever with me, and all that I have is "thine. Yel, it is meet that we rejoice, for "this thy brother was dead, and is alive again; "was lost, and is found!" Lord *George.* Yet had not the elder brother fome cause to be displeased, my good Mentoria? *Mentoria.* Not the least, my Lord, when we reflect, that forgiveness is a divine attribute, and that none stand in need of pardon, but thofe who have offended. As the elder brother's conduct had been unexceptionable, this virtue could not be exercised on him; it being necessary, there should be fome offence committed, before fore reconcilement can be sought, or obtained. The exclamation, which broke sorth from his father, manisested the emotions of his heart', and implied, he thought himself bound to'reward in the most ample manner the son, who had never given him ofsence. The concluding part of the sentence contains the lesson I wish to inculcate, namely, that we mould unseignedly rejoice in the advantages of others, and be instrumental in advancing their progress in virtue, or recovering them from error and delusion: that, so far from sounding our own praise on the desects or impersections of our friends, we should repair the tottering building, which sortified by sincerity and friendship, may constitute our strength; as the human species, like the vine, stands in need of a support. with-

out which neither would come to persec"tion, nor produce the fruits of virtue and abundance.

Lady *Mary. Ma/lers,* I think, is the next branch you are to consider. What kind of Respect, or Duty, do we owe to them?

Mentor ia.

Superiority, of whatever quality it consists, demands Respect, whether it proceeds from the possession of virtue, knowledge, or power,

K 4 ia in the superlative, or greatest, degree. Yow masters theresore are entitled to receive every mark, of attention you can possibly shew. You should never consider them as your equals, 'which will prevent any levity of conduct in their presence. You are all indispensably bound to attend to their instructions, which you will retain and profit by, if you acquire the habit of treating them with deserence and politeness. Lady *Louisa.*

I wish to know, how you would have us behave to pur *servants,* my dear Mentoria. *Mentoria.*

With humanity and condescension, you should always remember, notwithstanding they are your inseriors, they are your sellow-creatures; and in your conduct towards them, equally avoid haughtiness and familiarity. Maintain your own dignity, nor ever lofe it, by permitting a servant to joke with you, or partake of your recreations: such proceedings are not the effect of humility, but of a depraved taste, and meanness of spirit. There are some persons so sond of superiority, they choofe to associate with thofe who are beneath or dependent on them, sor no other reason, than the opportunity it affords them of gratifying their inclinations without control or reproach.

Lady

Lady *Mary.* We may command our servants, I suppose, to do every thing we like! *Mentoria.* This right, my dear Lady Mary, extends no farther than the bare discharge of their duty, and ought, to be exercised with caution and discretion. We should never lay an injunction on them, which appears not possible, or convenient for them to persorm; and be

ever ready to accept any reafonable excuse for the non-persormance. Let us in this, as in every other instance, incline to the side of mercy: let us break the bonds of servitude, and ease our dependents of their oppressive yoke. Lord *George.* How should we conduct ourselves to our *friends,* my dear Madam? *Mentoria.* We are ever inclined to persorm acts of kindness to thofe we style our friends. This duty is fo diffusive, and the motives fo numerous, which urge us to the discharge of it, there requires but little to be faid on this branch; more especially, as in a former discourse I enumerated the mutual obligations of friendship. I shall therefore proceed to point out the good.. will will we owe to the human species, without limitation or exception. The philanthropy J mean to recommend, is not only a Duty, but a Virtue: those who exercise it in the superlative degree, must possess benevolence, moderation, and steadiness; and be wholly exempt from arrogance, malice, or prejudices either personal or national: they must be inclined to redress the grievances of the distressed, camsort the afflicted, and clothe the naked; to which they should be alone impelled by the dictates of the Christian religion, and the sorce of their own seelings: neither should they wish or expect any reward, but what arises from the consciousness of having persormed their duty.

Lady *Alary.*

I imagine, my dear Mentoria, we are not required to be kind to the Jews! *Mentoria.*

Their religious sentiments would not excuse your failing to persorm any duty you owed them, as sellow-creatures. Their errors, though fatal in their tendency, demand our pity, as they were a desect ofjudgment. Our blessed Saviour prayed, that they might be sorgiven, as. they knew not what they did. Let us join in the fame requests request, and never persecute them. The parable of the good Samaritan affords us an excellent lesson of humanity, and also proves we should do good indiscriminately, and pay-no regard to the sect, or outward condition oi the object, whofe distresses excite our compassion. Lord *George.*

Why does this history particularly afford-us this lesson?

Mentoria.

Because the Jews and Samaritans were at such enmity, it was thought a capital offence to have the least intercourse: thus the woman of Samaria was surprised our Saviour should alk water of her, as he was a Jew. Lady *Mary.*

Then It was particularly good of the Samaritan, to take such care of the poor man in distress. You cannot imagine, my dear Mentoria, how much I admire his conduct! *Mentoria.*

He acted as every person ought to do, in the fame situation; which is, to persorm the service required, without any consideration of the advantages which would arise from, or the inconveniences that might attend it. Let us sollow his example, and bind up the wounds.- of ©f the afflicted, pouring in the balm of comfort and consolation. Let us ever practise the exhortation of our Saviour, delivered in these words: "Go, and do thou likewise." Which implies, we should seek an opportunity to testify our approbation of the Samaritan's conduct, by the convincing proof of imitation. "Let your light so shine besore men, that they may see your good works, and glorify your Father, who is in heaven!"

Lady *Louisa.*

Are there any other Duties, my good Mentoria?

Mentoria.

It is necessary, sor the good of the community, there should be subordination in the dis-, serent classes of mankind. I shall consider them under the heads of Superiority, Equality,, and Inseriority; which, I hope, will enable you to form a just conception of the-several states. Superiority requires the persons who possess it, to act with dignity and caution,

to. exercise their authority with moderation and justice, and to dispense their favours to thosewho appear most deserving of them. Lady *Louisa.*

What is our Duty to our Equals?

Mentoria.. Mentoria.

Like most other Duties, they are reciprocal,.and consist of a mutual exchange of kind osfices, and general good-will. As this state equally excludes prosound respect, and implicit obedience, it is necessary to point out the medium which should be preserved between these extremes, in order to make the cement of friendship binding. Undue familiarity proverbially produces contempt: we have also scriptural authority, where servile sear is, there can be no love, as love casteth out sear. From which it may be inserred, our deportment towards our Equals ought to be tinctured with the respect due to our Superiors, and the condescension and freedom authorized to our Inseriors; which is productive of the pleasing compound, usually.called *politeness.* Without the due observance of this amiable quality, the friendly intercourse of society degenerates into Barbarism and Incivility!

Lady *Mary.*

The state of Inseriority is the next branch you are to explain. I know, persons in that class are required to be obedient. *Mentoria.*

This obedience is limited, as they should ever avoid flattering the weakness and imperfections sections of their Superiors, and in all their. actions make a distinction between servility and respect. From the dependence of their state, it is necessary they should consorm to the will of their rulers, in every instance, which is not repugnant to reason or conscience. Lady *Mary.* But how will these rules regulate our conduct, my good Mentoria? *Mentoria.* You

must be actuated by the precept enjoined by our Saviour, "To do to others, as you "would they should do unto you. " You must theresore pursue the fame conduct to your Inseriors, as you would that your Superiors should to you; and pay the fame deserence to those above, as you expect to receive from thofe beneath you. To persons who are on a level with yourself, you should persorm such services, as seem most acceptable and necesfary to the sphere of lise in which you move. Be courteous to all; haughty and imperious to none. Be not high-minded, but condescend to thofe of low estate; and you will be respected by the great, and reverenced by the humble.

Excel,

Excel, and emulate thy parents praise.

Let thy intrinsic worth the fabric raise;

In every usesul art thy time employ,

Zealous to gain esteem, true heart-selt joy!

Attain each grace, that can adorn thy mind,

Blended with sentiment, and taste refin'd.

Envy can find no harbour in a breast,:

Th' abode, *l* trust, of peace, more welcome

guest,

Beatitude divine, and source of rest.

Neglect no duty, act with graceful ease,

Ever desire with modesty to please;

Let Virtue be thy guide, sor she'll dispense

Love, happiness, and raeek-ey'd innocence.

Oh! may she, kind to thee, her grace impart,

Never sorfake, deep rooted in thy heart!

r

CPSIA information can be obtained at www.ICGtesting.com
Printed in the USA
LVOW111418070613

337504LV00008B/211/P